# The Natural Selection of Autonomy

*SUNY Series, Philosophy and Biology*
*David Edward Shaner, Editor*

# THE NATURAL SELECTION OF AUTONOMY

*BRUCE N. WALLER*

*State University of New York Press*

Published by
State University of New York Press, Albany

© 1998  State University of New York

For information, address State University of New York Press,
State University Plaza, Albany, N.Y. 12246

Production by Diane Ganeles
Marketing by Nancy Farrell

Library of Congress Cataloging-in-Publication Data

Waller, Bruce N., 1946
    The natural selection of autonomy / Bruce N. Waller.
        p.    cm. — (SUNY series, philosophy and biology)
    Includes bibliographical references and index.
    ISBN 0-7914-3819-8 (hardcover : alk. paper). — ISBN 0-7914-3820-1
(pbk. : alk. paper)
    1. Autonomy (Philosophy)  2. Responsibility.  3. Biology-
-Philosophy.  4. Animal welfare.  5. Ethics, Evolutionary.
    I. Title.  II. Series: SUNY series in philosophy and biology.
    B808.67.W35  1998
    128—dc21                                                    97-37753
                                                                   CIP

10   9   8   7   6   5   4   3   2   1

For my schoolteacher mother, Lorena Norris Waller,
who dearly loved books, and who, God rest her soul,
would not have agreed with a word of this one.

# Contents

*Contents*

# Acknowledgments

This book developed out of several years of thinking and writing, and during that time I have received help and encouragement from many people. I am deeply grateful to all of them, though some—seeing the claims made in this book—may now repent themselves of their roles as co-conspirators.

The Department of Philosophy & Religious Studies at Youngstown State University has provided me a warm, stimulating, and wonderful work environment. Both colleagues and students have offered generous encouragement, trenchant criticisms, and fascinating ideas—often simultaneously. Special thanks to Chris Bache, Cynthia Brincat, Walter Carvin, Stephanie Dost-Barnhizer, Brendan Minogue, Mustansir Mir, Gabriel Palmer-Fernandez, Charles Reid, Tom Shipka, Mark Shutes, Donna Sloan, J.-C. Smith, Linda "Tess" Tessier, Larry Udell, and Robert Weaver. Also, every aspect of my work has been greatly aided by the phenomenal efficiency and unfailing good humor of our department secretary, Joan Bevan, and our student worker, Joan Iacobacci.

I have benefited from discussions with many people, so many that I'm sure I do not recall all of them; but those whose conversations and criticisms and encouragement were particularly helpful include Fred Alexander, Robert Kane, Jack Raver, George N. Schlesinger, and John G. Sullivan. Frequently their strong critiques of my views have pushed me to reformulate arguments and rethink my positions, and their genuine enthusiasm for the issues discussed has been a steady source of encouragement.

Richmond Campbell read a significant part of the manuscript in an earlier version, and his kind remarks as well as specific criticisms were particularly beneficial. Mark Bernstein, Richard Double, and George Graham all read the entire manuscript, and their comments were invaluable; and their conversations, correspondence, and their own philosophical writing—in both manuscript and final form—have for years had a strong positive influence on my work.

I am also grateful to the editors of *American Philosophical Quarterly*, *Analysis*, *Behavior and Philosophy*, *Biology and Philosophy*, and *Philosophia* for the opportunity to try out some of the arguments in this book, in earlier forms, in the pages of their journals.

My mother-in-law, Rose Newell, has often offered warm and encouraging words, which are most appreciated. My deepest gratitude is to my family: my wife, Mary, with whom I have discussed all of these ideas, and who has been a wonderful resource for information and ideas on current work in psychology, and most importantly a steady and certain source of affection and support; and my sons, Russell and Adam, who have not only enthusiastically discussed with me many of the ideas in this book, but have been constantly the most delightful and amazing and wonderful primates I have ever known.

# 1

---

## Introduction

Less than six centuries ago, humans were the fixed nucleus around which the planets, the Sun, the stars, and possibly the cherubims and seraphims daily revolved. Even Almighty God took an almost obsessive interest in our comings and goings. Copernicus nudged our earthly sphere off center stage, but humans remained the pride of God's creation: a little lower than the angels but crowned with honor and glory. By the time of Descartes, it was conceded that our bodies might be part of the mechanical world, but the human mental realm encompassing soul and rationality and limitless will set humans distinctly apart from the material realm and from the beasts. In the eighteenth century this special separation of humans came under vigorous attack from such philosophers as La Mettrie, Holbach, and Hume; but it was Darwin, a century later, who rooted humans firmly within the natural world amidst the other species. Humans have some marvelous characteristics—intricate social relations, a useful thumb, and we're clever with tools—but we are unequivocally animals. We evolved under the same forces that shape other species, and evolved from roots shared by very close cousins: humans are closer in evolutionary history and genetic makeup to chimpanzees than chimps are to gorillas or orangutans.

How shall we deal with this dramatic half-millennium of downward mobility? Three responses have been common. First, some cling to the wreckage, clutching whatever scraps of special status might keep them afloat. We may be largely the products of our evolutionary and conditioning histories, but we retain some small vital element of miracle-working power. Thus Roderick Chisholm insists that we can still exercise free choices that transcend our causal histories:

> If we are responsible . . . then we have a prerogative which some would attribute only to God: each of us, when we really act, is a prime mover unmoved. In doing what we do, we cause certain events to happen, and nothing and no one, except we ourselves, causes us to cause those events to happen. (1975, 395)

Richard Taylor asserts that each deliberative self-determining human is a "self-moving being" who can "cause an event to occur—namely, some act of his own—without anything else causing him to do so," and Taylor acknowledges that his "conception of men and their powers . . . is strange indeed, if not positively mysterious" (Taylor 1963, 52). And C. A. Campbell (1957) carves out a tiny niche of contra-causal free will in which we decide to exert or withhold the effort to rise to duty against tempting desires, and that special nonnatural power sustains humanity's exclusive title to free will and moral responsibility and genuine morality.

A second approach shares a basic premise with the first—saving autonomy and moral responsibility and genuine morality requires special powers beyond the natural—but draws the opposite conclusion: free will (and moral responsibility and knowledge of genuine morality) are antiquated vestiges of pre-scientific (or at least pre-Darwinian) thought, and they must be banished. Thus B. F. Skinner (1971, 200) asserts that "autonomous man is a device used to explain what we cannot explain in any other way. He has been constructed from our ignorance, and as our understanding increases, the very stuff of which he is composed vanishes." John Hospers claims that, on deeper examination of human behavior, the notion of autonomy disappears, and "'Right' and 'wrong' . . . have no meaning here either" (1958, 141). E. O. Wilson agrees, proclaiming that "the time has come for ethics to be removed temporarily from the hands of the philosophers and biologicized" (1975, 562).

A third response has gained favor among contemporary philosophers. It may strike some as a philosophical version of whistling past the graveyard, in this case, past the graveyard of the miracle-working powers that propped up the special human capacities for morality, autonomy, and moral responsibility. This is the response of compatibilism: when we fully grasp the implications of contemporary natural science (including Darwinism), we recognize that a thoroughly scientific Darwinian naturalism can be reconciled with the uniqely human powers that enable humans and humans alone to act morally (or immorally), live autonomously (or heteronomously), and be morally responsible (and justly deserving of reward or retribution).

This book champions a fourth response. Autonomy and morality remain vitally important to natural human animals. They must not be discarded along with the mysteries and miracles, for they require no such props. But when humans and human behavior plunge out of the angelic realm and land on earth amidst the other animals, the fall does have a profound impact. The simple hopes of the compatibilists—nothing philosophically important has changed, and our views of free will and moral responsibility and morality require little revision— cannot be sustained. We remain autonomous moral animals, but with important differences: first and foremost, we must share our moral world with other species.

Darwinian naturalism challenges the traditional philosophical assumption of human exclusivity for autonomy and morality. If autonomy and morality are useful adaptations (rather than god-given or self-made mysteries), then it is likely that other animals evolved similar autonomous and moral behavioral adaptations in response to similar environments. By rejecting schemes to guarantee a human monopoly on autonomy and morality, we can examine them writ large in the natural world we share with other animals.

# 2

---

## Natural Autonomy and
## Alternative Possibilities

Autonomy requires open choices, alternative possibilities, viable options. Or so it seems. However, attempts to give an account of such open-choices-autonomy have encountered notorious difficulties. Libertarian theories became enmeshed in the inscrutable mysteries of an agency that transcends natural causes,[1] and the compatibilist attempts to reconcile autonomy with naturalism (or determinism) have a strong scent of ad hoc desperation. As a result, many empiricist philosophers have turned away from autonomy-as-alternatives in favor of autonomy-as-authenticity. The most dramatic example is offered by Harry Frankfurt: the willing addict has no alternatives and cannot do otherwise, but because he decisively favors his addiction Frankfurt judges him free and fully autonomous. Thus open alternatives are not required for autonomy, and autonomy-as-authenticity supplants autonomy-as-alternatives.

Frankfurt's willing addict is designed to drive a stake through the heart of autonomy-as-alternatives: the willing addict has no options but is still autonomous. And indeed the addict *is* doing as he wishes, and even wills as he wishes; but he certainly does not enjoy "all the freedom it is possible to desire or conceive" (1971, 17). The poor devil whose hopes and possibilities and alternatives have constricted into a single-minded desire for drugs is at best a happy slave. This slave has lost all hope of escape, and his only remaining desire is perfect and single-minded service to his master. He is profoundly—some might say *authentically*—a slave; but no one should imagine that he is autonomous.[2]

But is he "authentically" a slave? Problems with determining the self's *authentic* wishes have led some philosophers to reinforce authenticity with Reason. Thus Susan Wolf argues that an agent really wants the ability "to 'track' the True and Good in her value judgments" (1990, 75); thus the "freedom" to choose some other alternative is a pseudofreedom that "no one could ever have reason to want to exercise" (1990, 55). As on Frankfurt's view, alternative possibilities are unnecessary; indeed, they are undesirable, supplanted by the *True* self's authentic quest for the straight and narrow path to the *Good*.

Notwithstanding Wolf's spirited defense of rational single-path authenticity, there is something disquieting about having no alternative to the one true path dictated by Reason. Reason may be a better master than drugs, but such straight and narrow authenticity is still troubling. The concern was voiced by Dostoyevsky's underground man:

> So one's own free, unrestrained choice, one's own whim, be it the wildest, one's own fancy, sometimes worked up to a frenzy—that is the most advantageous advantage that cannot be fitted into any table or scale and that causes every system and every theory to crumble into dust on contact. And where did these sages pick up the notion that man must have something that they feel is a normal and virtuous set of wishes; what makes them think that man's will must be reasonable and in accordance with his own interests? All man actually needs is independent will, at all costs and whatever the consequences. (1864/1910, 110)

One need not share Dostoyevsky's frenzy to share his visceral sense of loss at Reason's denial of alternative possibilities. There are powerful causes and sufficient reasons for fearing the loss of open alternatives, and a Darwinian perspective reveals them clearly. Compatibilists are justified in rejecting mysterious libertarian versions of autonomy-as-alternatives; but when compatibilists (like Frankfurt and Wolf) abandon alternatives in favor of reflective optionless authenticity, they throw out the baby with the bath water.

Alternative possibilities are essential to autonomy, but the place to seek autonomy-as-alternatives is in the natural biological world, rather than in mysterious libertarian agency. Alternative possibilities must be rescued from the libertarians, brought down to earth, and thoroughly naturalized. A good place to start the naturalization process is on a foraging expedition with a white-footed mouse.

## Autonomy Naturalized

While studying the behavior of feral white-footed mice that had learned to run through mazes for rewards, J. Lee Kavanau noted that well-educated mice—quite familiar with the correct path to food—occasionally take the wrong route:

> Investigators sometimes are puzzled by the fact that once an animal has learned a discrimination well, it nonetheless still makes some "incorrect" responses. Actually, these responses are incorrect only from the point of view of the investigator's rigidly prescribed program, not from that of the animal. The basis for these responses is that the animal has a certain degree of variability built into many of its behavior patterns. This variability is adaptive to conditions in the wild, where there are many relationships that are not strictly prescribed. (1967, 1628)[3]

Thus if the white-footed mouse never strayed from the one true path, she would miss the opportunities that might subsequently appear along other routes and would be ill-equipped to respond rapidly should her most beneficial route be closed off or run dry. By occasionally taking alternative paths, the white-footed mouse keeps her options open. Kavanau summarizes the benefits:

> The habit of deviating fairly frequently from stereotyped "correct" responses, together with a high level of spontaneous activity, underlie the remarkable facility with which white-footed mice can be taught to cope with complex contingencies. (1967, 1628)

The spontaneous white-footed mouse may not be the paradigm of autonomy, but she can teach us some important autonomy lessons. Our success—in gaining knowledge, pursuing science, working out problems—is deeply rooted in the pattern that also guides the foraging of the white-footed mouse. We pursue a path because it is particularly successful, but we do not stop exploring new ones. When the successful behavioral pattern loses its effectiveness, we have other alternatives ready. In like manner, we do not entirely abandon the previously successful pattern and may return to it occasionally (though we know it is unlikely to work). If later the old behavioral pattern again proves beneficial, we are less likely to overlook those benefits.

The same pattern of maintaining alternatives can be observed in behavior (of pigeons, mice, and humans) shaped on a variable interval reinforcement schedule (the schedule that shapes most of our learned behavior). Behavior shaped on a variable interval schedule can be maintained with very limited positive reinforcement; and when the pattern is almost extinguished, one instance of positive reinforcement revives it to near full strength. That is not invariably a good thing: it causes my deleterious gambling behavior—almost ended by a long losing streak—to regain full intensity following one small payoff. But the overall advantage of having a large range of behavior readily available for changing environments and new contingencies more than balances the disadvantages—for white-footed mice as well as humans.

Thus autonomy-as-alternatives is grounded in learning strategies that are not the exclusive province of higher-level rational powers, nor the exclusive property of humans. Autonomy involves access to genuine alternatives, and in that sense human autonomy parallels white-footed mouse autonomy. Human intelligence generates important differences between the autonomy of white-footed mice and the autonomy of humans, but the differences are best understood by examining their common roots in the exploration of alternative paths. The white-footed mouse explores alternative paths with keen scent and sharp eyes and swift feet. Our reflective analytic intelligence is our best exploratory device, and without it we are as ill-equipped for examining a variety of paths and behavioral patterns as would be a white-footed mouse deprived of scent and sight. So reason is essential to full human autonomy: reason opens a wide range of possibilities and options and facilitates careful assessment of those options.

This use of reason to discover and explore and maintain open alternatives stands in stark contrast to the more traditional use of Reason (favored by Kant and Susan Wolf) to discover the single true path. The former plants reason firmly in the natural world, as a natural extension of animal intelligence; the latter makes Reason a special faculty for discovery of final immutable truths. The former keeps options open for use in a changing world; the latter locks onto a single true path, from which any deviation is either unfortunate error or shallow impetuosity.

Susan Wolf develops the most impressive contemporary account of single-path-Reason, and on her view it does seem absurd to wish for the possibility of swerving: it would be like judging a train better because it can occasionally jump the tracks. But Wolf's Kantian Reason perspective is too short. If the focus is exclusively on the most immediately desirable path, the option of pursuing a less desirable alternative seems at best a bothersome distraction, at worst a perilous and irrational mistake, and in any case *not* an enriching freedom. As Wolf disparages autonomy-as-alternatives:

> To want autonomy, then, is not only to want the ability to make choices even when there is no basis for choice but to want the ability to make choices on no basis even when a basis exists. But the latter ability would seem to be an ability no one could ever have reason to want to exercise. Why would one want the ability to pass up the apple when to do so would merely be unpleasant or arbitrary? (1990, 55)

From the perspective of natural autonomy-as-alternatives, one might want to pass up the apple (the most desirable and "reasonable" option) in order to discover new sources of fruit. After all, the apple harvest will eventually be exhausted. This longer perspective emphasizes pursuing the optimum pattern of results in a changing world fraught with uncertainty. That pattern is not bound to the single path that seems currently most promising.[4]

## Autonomy in the Natural World

Natural intelligent autonomy—autonomy-as-alternatives—is our best strategy for rich and successful survival. It reconciles spontaneous exploration with intelligent reflection, while avoiding libertarian mysteries and authenticity muddles. But can such an autonomy of open possibilities exist in a natural (or a determined) world?

The natural world is exactly the place for an autonomy of alternative possibilities. Our "survival strategy" has shaped us, like our mammalian relative the white-footed mouse, to keep our options open. We might have evolved like the insects, with rigidly programmed behavioral patterns. Our evolutionary process took a different tack: we are "programmed" to favor a variety of paths and to maintain such possibilities even when one path is the most immediately beneficial. This inclination is shared by many other species,[5] it is explicable in natural terms, and its development and functioning no more require mysterious libertarian nonnatural creativity than does the evolution of the hand.

If it is difficult to picture how autonomy-as-alternatives works in the natural nonmiraculous world, that is because autonomy-as-alternatives has long been associated with mysterious nonnatural *libertarian* choices: choices that set humans miraculously *apart* from the natural environment. In contrast to natural autonomy-as-alternatives, the libertarian principle of open alternative possibilities was designed to do heavier work than simply keeping options open: libertarian transcendent free will struggles with the burden of moral responsibility, and bearing that burden does require nonnatural miraculous choices. As described by C. A. Campbell, a champion of libertarian autonomy, the libertarian choice between the paths of moral effort and moral lethargy is "something for which a man is responsible without qualification, something that is not affected by heredity and environment but depends solely upon the self itself" (Campbell 1957, 169).

Naturalism cannot support such unqualified choices, so compatibilists—who want a *natural* autonomy-as-alternatives that can still support moral responsibility—proposed a "hypothetical" account of "could have acted/chosen otherwise," which Campbell describes thus:

> . . . All that we really require to be assured of, in order to justify our holding X morally responsible for an act, is, we are told [by compatibilists], that X could have acted otherwise if he had chosen otherwise (Moore, Stevenson); or perhaps that X could have acted otherwise . . . if he had been placed in different circumstances. (Campbell 1957, 161)

Campbell cogently argues that such hypothetical interpretations of "could have acted otherwise" cannot carry the weight of moral responsibility. But if we bid good riddance to moral responsibility (as will be recommended in chapter 4) and leave it with libertarian free will—and with the angels and miracles and mysteries in the only environment in which moral responsibility can survive[6]—then the hypothetical interpretation of "could have acted otherwise" provides precisely what we want.

Campbell (and Richard Taylor and Roderick Chisholm) require alternatives that cannot be explained naturalistically, choices that are explicable only by appeal to my own ultimate creative self-willed powers: the decisive choice must be mine (not ultimately the product of my environment) if I am to be morally responsible and justly deserve blame or reward. But such libertarian alternative choices—choices exercised independently of the environment—corrupt the natural value of alternative possibilities. As products of our natural environment, we want alternatives shaped by their long-term or short-term usefulness in the environment in which we live, alternatives available for selection in *response* to our changing environment. The sterile insulated libertarian alternatives required by moral responsibility are not shaped by the environmental forces to which we must respond effectively. To the contrary, libertarian choices *must* be isolated from environmental influences: libertarian choices must be something for which I am "responsible without qualification" and thus "not affected by heredity or environment." But *natural* autonomy-as-alternatives (as practiced by humans as well as white-footed mice) is tightly linked to environmental shaping.

When pursuit of alternatives is recognized as an effective *natural* strategy—for mice as well as humans—then the compatibilist "hypothetical" account of alternatives becomes more appealing. We do not want freedom for choices with no causal antecedents, freedom from all environmental contingencies, freedom to make inexplicable choices. To the contrary, what we want is precisely what Campbell disparages: we (humans and white-footed mice) want to be able to act otherwise *if* we choose otherwise; that is, we want other options available when we experience different circumstances in our changing environment. The white-footed mouse chooses to follow path A, and does so; but she wants to be able to follow paths B and C and D also, when she chooses: she wants to keep those alternative paths open. The choice made is the result of complex environmental influences, including the long-term environmental history that shaped the species to occasionally explore different paths. The choice nonetheless meets the white-footed mouse autonomy requirements: not a choice independent of all natural influences, but instead one of many open alternatives that can be followed in a changing environment under "different circumstances."

In like manner, natural human autonomy does not require causally inexplicable miraculous choosing. What we require is the opportunity to take a different path in different conditions, the capacity to intelligently consider and pursue other possibilities when a changing world makes an old path less rewarding. In order to keep such possibilities open, we must occasionally make specific path choices that are not immediately optimum. Perhaps that is what gives mysterious libertarian choice its enduring appeal. But there is nothing mysterious about the alternative choices required by natural autonomy. They optimize alternative possibilities, which is important for successful living in our changing natural world. Thus when examined from a wider perspective—a perspective encompassing the pattern of alternative-preserving choices—any residual mystery disappears, and autonomy-as-alternatives flourishes in the natural environment.

A clearer understanding of natural autonomy-as-alternatives distinguishes it from libertarian accounts of contra-causal alternatives, and also highlights what has been left out of many contemporary *compatibilist* accounts of autonomy that reject autonomy-as-alternatives. Contrary to Frankfurt, concern over the loss of alternative possibilities is well-placed. Consider Frankfurt's famous example (1969, 835–836) of the villain, Black, who wants Jones to perform a certain action. Jones imagines he can perform that action or not, as he wishes; but Jones is mistaken, for Black is closely monitoring Jones, and should Jones choose some action other than the one Black wishes, Black would manipulate Jones' brain to compel Jones to perform Black's bidding. So Jones really has no alternatives. Still, Jones performs the act of his own volition, and Black intervenes not at all. Surely, Frankfurt argues, the act is still Jones' act (even though he had no other possibilities), and Jones is autonomous and morally responsible.

Jones is not, however, autonomous; he only imagines himself to be so. Indeed, his loss of autonomy is exacerbated rather than ameliorated by his ignorance of Black's machinations. Not only are his alternative paths blocked, but also his understanding of them is distorted. Human autonomy is enhanced by intelligent reflective consideration of alternatives (our intelligence is the distinctive autonomy-enhancing power of humans, analogous to the speed or sense of smell of other animals); but intelligent reflection is not autonomy-enhancing if it operates under deception. Thus when an individual (such as Frankfurt's willing addict, who cannot do otherwise) is deprived of alternatives, but still acts as he genuinely wants to act, he may be acting "authentically"—but not autonomously. If he believes he has alternatives and does not (because some trickster has closed them off), then he is even further from autonomy: he lacks alternatives, and lacks the knowledge that is the human's best tool for discovering and exploring alternatives.[7]

Natural human autonomy involves the use of intelligent analysis and critical reflection to explore and choose among alternatives. It requires not only an environment that offers options and opportunities, but also the critical capacities to recognize and analyze those options. It is more efficient to think about, study, and discuss a variety of possible paths instead of physically trudging down them.[8] Reason broadens human alternatives and autonomy, just as foot speed enhances white-mouse autonomy. Thus an individual whose reflective powers are shackled by childhood guilt (or jealousy or obsessions or false beliefs) has severe autonomy impediments. The man whose choices are controlled by an unrecognized sibling jealousy (a jealousy that inhibits his ability to adequately consider alternatives[9]) suffers impairment of autonomy. The natural autonomy-as-alternatives account explains such autonomy impairments without the cumbersome explanatory machinery of hierarchical authenticity. Our autonomy is limited when we are prevented—by early childhood traumas or unresolved sibling rivalries or long-term poverty or whatever—from intelligently exploring alternatives. And our autonomy is limited when we lack the intelligence or energy or self-control techniques to effectively pursue options in which we are interested (if I want to write my dissertation but cannot overcome my lethargy or writer's block or video game obsession, I suffer restricted opportunities and reduced autonomy). Explaining such autonomy limitations does not require a true authentic self, revealed or confirmed by decisive higher-order reflective willing. Quite simply, human autonomy suffers from impaired intelligence in the same way that white-footed mouse autonomy suffers from a sprained ankle.

This does not imply that we must keep all our options open and continue to make occasional forays down every possible path. Alternatives that consistently yield no benefits will eventually be entirely avoided, as the behavior of following that path is finally extinguished; the research program that sinks deeper into degeneration (Lakatos 1978) is ultimately abandoned. The white-footed mouse who occasionally dashes headlong into a brick wall (to keep that behavioral option open, in case the bricks should one day dissolve and open the way to a white-footed mouse cornucopia) does not enlarge her autonomy. Autonomy does require genuine alternatives; but autonomy is enhanced by selective intelligent consideration of alternatives, rather than indiscriminate multiplication of alternative paths.

When autonomy is understood as open exploration of alternatives, then appeals to such shadowy substances as the "authentic self" can be eliminated. Defining the authentic true self (without appeals to mysterious libertarian free will or God's purpose for our lives) is notoriously difficult. Natural autonomy-as-alternatives avoids such difficulties and focuses attention on effective intelligent choice: a natural—and naturally explicable—extension of the exploration of alternatives that has proved its value for many species. Quandaries about "authenticity" and "true selves" wither away. If I am making an intelligent and knowledgeable choice among a wide range of open alternative paths, there is nothing further that "authenticity" could contribute to my autonomy. (There remains an important role for *natural* authenticity, to be discussed in the following chapter, but that is not the "one true path" authenticity of the "true self.")

The key to autonomy (natural autonomy-as-alternatives) is not some authentic or miraculous act of choice, but instead the total choice context. To see genuine natural autonomy one must avoid the easy myopic focus on the choice itself. The question is not how resounding or beneficial or thoroughly self-approved the choice may be. Determining whether the choice is naturally *autonomous* requires study of the setting in which the choice is made, with focus on two key questions: are there genuine alternatives available and does the individual possess what is needed to effectively examine those alternatives (human needs include knowledge, intelligence, and freedom from obsession or irrational fear; white-footed mice require swift feet and keen scent along with intelligence). It is not the decisiveness of the choice that establishes autonomy, but the richness of the choosing context: a context that includes both individual abilities and environmental options.

Naturalized autonomy breaks the barrier between human autonomy and the behavior of other species—and it also blurs any sharp lines between free will and autonomy. Some may object that naturalized autonomy is at best an account of operating with free will, when one's will is not shackled by constraint or coercion or obsession. But autonomy—they might continue—is something different, and more exalted: autonomy requires being a law unto oneself, judging and legislating the rules and values of one's own life. Such a distinction is designed to maintain the radical difference between humans and other animals, a difference that the naturalized autonomy view represents as points on a continuum rather than a basic difference-in-kind. Humans are distinctively rule-makers and law-givers; but rather than viewing that unique capacity as a means of completely separating human autonomous behavior from the rest of the animal world, it is more economical to understand it as a distinctive human enhancement of option-enlarging autonomy, an especially powerful enhancement but still analogous to autonomy enhancements enjoyed by other species.

Autonomous rule-giving is a way of enhancing options and opportunities, not a difference-in-kind from free will. Higher reflective capacities are an important adaptation, but they no more set humans apart as the exclusively autonomous species than does the cheetah's option-enhancing swiftness give him a special proprietary claim on autonomy. Of course one can stipulate that only rule-giving makes one special and autonomous; but such overemphasis on what is humanly distinct obscures real and important connections with other species.

When we move beyond a narrow obsessive focus on *human* autonomy to examine autonomy in a richer and wider range of animal behavior, then the mysteries vanish and the complications diminish, and it is comparatively easy to see the simple natural value of animal autonomy—including an important natural role for authenticity. Authenticity was treated rather harshly in earlier sections, with autonomy-as-alternatives shoving authenticity aside. The following chapter explores a naturalized authenticity, that complements—rather than competes with—autonomy-as-alternatives.

# 3

---

## Natural Authenticity

Authenticity of the "true self" is different from autonomy and stems from a different tradition. Autonomy is the good of a changing and evolving environment, where keeping our options open is a valuable survival tool in the face of variable resources, new opportunities, and uncertain conditions. Authenticity, in contrast, is designed for a permanent static world: we are authentic when we are following the single true path ordained by the God whose artifacts we are. That God—whether the God of Moses or of Aristotle—changes not, so keeping one's options open is not a virtue; to the contrary, perfect authenticity demands perfect obedience (to the eternal laws of God or the immutable laws of Reason).

Even among such naturalist advocates of authenticity as Frankfurt, authenticity works best when isolated from the changing circumstances of environmental causation. The truly authentic character makes a "decisive commitment" (Frankfurt 1971, 16) to a single path or volition; and at that level, the environmental forces that shaped the commitment cannot be considered: it is decisively and finally and authentically my choice, no matter how it came about. Authenticity thus focuses attention on the end, the conclusive act of choosing. The authentic individual follows the true path, or makes the decisive resounding commitment, and there is little or no concern about how the true path or the decisive commitment was reached.

The "authentic true self" is a vestige of humans as God's artifacts and cannot be part of a naturalist-Darwinian account of autonomous behavior. Nonetheless, there is something in authenticity that is of genuine value in the natural world—not an authenticity guaranteeing ultimate independence of the world that shapes us, but rather an authenticity that expands and enhances our effective responses to the rich evolving variety of that world. The value of autonomy-as-alternatives was the subject of the previous chapter: We (along with many other animals) want and need the freedom to do otherwise, to pursue a variety of open alternatives. Still, we also admire the steadfast autonomous commitment of "here I stand; I cannot do otherwise." We feel the charm of Susan Wolf's authentic single-path pursuit of the True and the Good, but we are not deaf to the plaint of Dostoyevsky's underground man:

> So one's own free, unrestrained choice, one's own whim, be it the wildest, one's own fancy, sometimes worked up to a frenzy—that is the most advantageous advantage that cannot be fitted into any table or scale and that causes every system and every theory to crumble into dust on contact.(1864/1961, 110)

After careening between these conflicting models it is not surprising that some adopt Thomas Nagel's desolate View from Nowhere (1986, 110ff.): we can neither abandon nor harmonize these different perspectives; thus the problem is intractable. Or we might accept the analysis proposed by Richard Double (1991): our notion of autonomy is governed by competing inconsistent paradigms; thus there is no truth of the matter about autonomy, and instead we must recognize the nonreality of free will.

It is possible to resolve this struggle. Autonomy-as-alternatives and authenticity (natural authenticity, not the "true self" variety) do not conflict, but are instead different aspects of a unified natural autonomy. They require neither miracles nor mysteries for their realization, and we can examine them both in their natural symbiotic state: writ large in society, writ small in individual learning histories, and writ deep into our biological nature.

To unite autonomy-as-alternatives with authenticity we must first be clear about what we are linking. No adhesive will join Dostoyevsky's capricious underground man to Susan Wolf's single-narrow-path disciple of the True and Good. The bond must instead be forged between more modest—and more natural—versions of autonomy-as-alternatives and authenticity. As already noted, autonomy-as-alternatives is not caprice, nor does it require miraculous freedom from environmental influences and past causal history. To the contrary, it is rooted deep in our natural history and in the mundane behavior of many species. To see how naturalized authenticity complements—rather than conflicts with—natural autonomy-as-alternatives, consider the fox of folk song fame: the one that goes out on a chase one night. If farmer John's duck pen has been bountiful this season, the fox may visit it more often than not; but Reynard will occasionally pursue other paths as well, keeping those options open in case a tasty mouse family moves into the neighborhood, and sometimes visiting formerly-plentiful-but-now-barren hunting grounds (farmer Ben's poultry farm is no longer in operation; but if it should resume business, the fox—by pursuing a variety of paths and keeping-its-options-open—will soon know). Rigid adherence to the currently optimal "one true path" would fail to inform the fox of other food sources, and would leave Reynard no promising options should farmer John erect a fox-proof fence. So there are good natural grounds for favoring open possibilities—natural advantages for mice, foxes, and humans—and thus our fondness for autonomy-as-alternatives runs deep: deeper than our higher rational planning powers, though not in conflict with them. (Not all species pursue autonomy-as-alternatives, as the "sphexish" behavior of digger wasps (Dennett 1984, 10ff.) reminds us. But species whose evolutionary survival strategy favored contingency-shaped learning above rigid behavioral programming will value autonomy-as-alternatives.)

What happens when farmer John closes his duck operation and focuses exclusively on wheat farming? The autonomous fox finds the pickings slim at John's duck pen; but—here emerges autonomy-as-authenticity—the faithful fox does not abandon that path altogether. If the duck pen has long been a source of delicious ducks for the fox family, Reynard will continue to visit Farmer John long after the ducks have disappeared. Eventually the fox ventures to Farmer John's less frequently; but if a subsequent visit produces a duck, that single positive reinforcement will restore Reynard's duck pen visiting to full strength. If ducks are discovered sporadically over a long period, Reynard will become dedicated to visiting John's duck pen and may persist in such visits through a lengthy period of futility. Reynard is committed to visiting Farmer John: his duck pen jaunts are authentically his own.

Reynard's authenticity may not run as deep as some might wish. Suppose one asks: but was the fox really an authentic devotee of Farmer John's duck pen? Wasn't that just a behavior shaped by the environmental contingencies that our fox happened to encounter? Maybe he was authentically a gentle vegetarian fox, drawn into duck pilfering against his true nature. Such questions end in a metaphysical morass of god-given selves. The fox has no given true nature (other than what is given by long-term genetic and short-term learning histories) against which to mark approximations to or deviations from "genuine authenticity." Reynard is an authentic fancier of Farmer John's ducks; he is so because of the various factors—both biological and learned—that shaped him; and there is no deeper depth to plumb, whether in foxes or humans. What has been shaped is all there is.

This account of authenticity stays snugly within the naturalistic framework; nonetheless, it is at home in both the gritty, gamey pursuits of the fox and in the sublime human pursuit of knowledge. Just as the fox does not abandon Farmer John's duck pen when the duck supply runs thin, so neither does the scientist abandon a cherished and productive theory when the results prove discouraging. Practicing scientists cling to theories in the face of strong counter-evidence and despite "refutation" by crucial experiments. Thomas Kuhn (1962) recognized that this is not only common but useful to the scientific enterprise. If perfectly detached scientists lightly relinquished theories when encountering problems or failed predictions, they would prematurely abandon theories that might ultimately prove their worth. Natural authenticity emphasizes that this process is not unique to scientific practice: it can be observed in foxes and pigeons, mice and men, philosophers and scientists. Our commitments are not immediately discarded when conditions change, new evidence appears, and winds shift. And it is in such commitments—rooted in mundane, nonmysterious, useful behavioral patterns—that we find the substance of natural authenticity.

This is not to suggest that all our authentic value commitments were shaped like Reynard's allegiance to Farmer John's duck pen. (Neither, of course, are all of Reynard's: his commitment to his pups, for example, was shaped by much longer-term processes.) My commitment to Marxism is the product of reading and reflection and conversation, rather than a simple series of immediate reinforcements in the presence of Marxist ideas (though one need not dismiss the effects of complex learned reinforcers—new insights, rushes of recognition—shaping dedication to the Marxist perspective). The point is that authenticity and commitment (commitment not totally under the sway of immediate circumstances) is naturally useful and not a mysterious nor uniquely human phenomenon.

When natural authenticity is fleshed out, the conflict with autonomy-as-alternatives disappears: they perform different but complementary functions. Autonomy-as-alternatives keeps options open, enlarging opportunities in a changing environment. Authenticity keeps options open when immediate conditions would prompt their abandonment. We require autonomy-as-alternatives, and exploration of alternatives, even when one path seems thoroughly satisfactory; but we also require authenticity, for it maintains paths and commitments as viable options when they are unproductive in the short term. Such loyalty-authenticity maintains a richer range for autonomy-as-alternatives.

But can this natural authenticity be an adequate account of human authenticity? Isn't Reynard's "authenticity" too shallow to be placed under the same rubric with the authenticity of a reflective, deliberative human being? After all, human authenticity involves more than desiring to preserve a certain pathway; it also involves the capacity to reflectively deliberate about one's full hierarchy of desires and considered preferences. As in Frankfurt's famous case, the authentic human may desire drugs, and may reflectively wish to desire drugs, and may "metareflectively" will to wish to desire drugs. And while there are limits to the human capacity for such hierarchical reflection—anything beyond three levels is more philosophical fancy than psychological reality—those limits still far outstrip Reynard's reflective reaches. The fox may desire to explore Farmer John's duck pen, and that desire may eventually weaken and extinguish, or weaken and revive; but Reynard does not reflect on whether he desires to desire such exploration, or on whether he prefers that those desires wither or flourish. Such hierarchical reflection is as far beyond Reynard as is reflection on the moral justification for liberating ducks from Farmer John. Even a shrewd and resourceful Reynard will lack the capacity—the conceptual and language capacity, for a start—required for such hierarchical authenticity-establishing reflection. And if it is nonsense to suggest that Reynard could reflectively approve or disapprove of his desire to reconnoiter Farmer John's duck pen, it is nonsense on stilts to imagine Reynard reflectively affirming or regretting his reflective wish to desire Farmer John's ducks. Hierarchical reflection forms the core of contemporary authenticity accounts; and—the objection goes—if that core is absent from natural authenticity, then natural "authenticity" must be different-in-kind from (and thus an inadequate explanation of) human authenticity.

The answer to this objection makes clearer the nature of natural authenticity, and its deep affinities with even the highly intellectualized authenticity of the hierarchical theorists. Hierarchical authenticity is not different-in-kind from Reynard's natural authenticity. Human reflective hierarchical authenticity is a more sophisticated and specially adaptive version of Reynard's authenticity, and to understand human reflective authenticity, we must first appreciate the functioning of natural authenticity at the more basic level shared by humans and foxes.

Reynard's authentic desire to visit Farmer John functions to keep that path open during periods when the positive reinforcements of the duck variety are dwindling and the immediate conditions do not favor the path to Farmer John's. Human hierarchical authenticity serves the same alternative-enhancing function, but in a more complex manner that yields special advantages. Reynard wants to seek Farmer John's ducks, and it will generally be useful to Reynard to sustain that desire— and keep that option open—during periods of scant or no immediate benefits. Reynard's authenticity, limited as it may be, serves that useful purpose. Regina wants to write philosophy articles. She is a successful writer and is sustained through effective positive reinforcers: as she works she gains enriching insights, her colleagues praise her work, journals send reinforcing acceptance letters, and she enjoys reviewing her own well-crafted work. But then Regina hits a slump: journals reject her submissions, her colleagues misunderstand her new work, her computer crashes and consumes the only copy of her most recent essay. Frustrations mount, positive reinforcements gutter, and Farmer John's duck pen—or its article-writing analogue—appears empty and deserted. But Regina persists, just as Reynard does.

Eventually Reynard's behavior of trotting to the duck pen

will extinguish; and so may Regina's article writing, of course. But Regina has special capacities for keeping that option open, hierarchical capacities that are beyond Reynard. If writing philosophy articles is deeply authentic for Regina, she worries when she recognizes the withering away of her immediate desire to write philosophy. When she finds her desire to write philosophy superseded by her desire to vegetate in front of the television, she is disturbed. She now desires to watch television more than she desires to write philosophy, but she certainly does not reflectively wish to so desire. That level is unavailable to Reynard; but because it is available to reflective Regina, she can deliberately take steps to sustain and revitalize her philosophy writing—to keep that option open—long beyond the time when it might have otherwise extinguished. She can call a colleague who appreciates and encourages her work; or she could give postdated checks to a friend, with instructions to mail the checks to some villainous politician's election campaign unless Regina completes a set number of pages each week. Through such strategies Regina will be pushed to write, and then other contingencies—the praise of a colleague, acceptance by a journal, or the satisfying solution to some vexing problem—are likely to revive and sustain her work. Regina's hierarchical authenticity is not functionally different from Reynard's more basic version: they are both natural means of keeping commitment-alternatives open when they would otherwise disappear. But Regina's hierarchical authenticity offers greater resources for fulfilling that function, and can sustain behavior through deeper duress in more hostile environments.

## Decisive Commitments and Willing Addicts

Reynard's natural authenticity is cut from the same functional cloth as human reflective hierarchical authenticity, and recognition of that connection offers the solution to problems that plague hierarchical authenticity accounts. I want X, and I am pleased that I want X, and I reflectively approve of being pleased that I want X; but where does it end? Must I metareflectively approve of reflectively approving my pleasure in wanting X? It appears that of the reflective approval of approving there is no end, and "all is vanity and vexation of spirit." To stop the regress, Frankfurt posits a high level "resounding commitment" that is disquietingly similar to libertarian "miraculous choice." But the natural authenticity account requires no inexplicable "resounding commitment"; rather, there is a naturally explicable wish to keep a formerly beneficial path open despite strong immediate contrary environmental circumstances. And instead of an enigmatic "final resounding commitment," there is simply a natural limit on the reflective authenticity resources available for this task.

Natural authenticity ranges easily over both Reynard's duck-seeking and Regina's higher-order will-to-write, and it demystifies problems of "highest level resounding commitments." Furthermore, natural authenticity can resolve the most vexing challenge to traditional compatibilist authenticity accounts: the happy slave or—in Frankfurt's dramatic case—the willing addict. So long as the addict longs to be free of addiction, the hierarchical account goes swimmingly: the addict is not free and does not act authentically because his higher-order reflective willing rejects his desire for drugs. But when the addict affirms and reflectively favors addiction, then the hierarchical theory counts him a free and authentic addict. In one of Gerald Dworkin's striking examples (1976, 25) the person who longs to become a great skier due to envy—but who despises his obsessive envy—is not free and authentic. However, should he recognize and reflectively approve his envious motive, then he is transformed into a free and authentic puppet of his envy.

Frankfurt's willing addict and Dworkin's willingly envious skier are dramatic examples, but we can find more pedestrian—and perhaps more disturbing—cases. Consider the factory worker who chafes in an environment of mindless repetitive labor while longing for work that involves thought, creativity, and decision making. Such a laborer is an unfortunate, unfree, and unauthentic victim (as Frankfurt and Dworkin correctly emphasize). But when the laborer's desire to think and plan and choose is finally killed by exhausting, mind-numbing drudgery, then the laborer has achieved authenticity in her regimented role. Another example: the woman who struggles against a culturally defined subservient role is not free; but the woman whose subjugation has been so thorough as to extinguish any wish for independence is free and authentic.

Certainly it is possible to cling to the hierarchical analysis when faced with such paradox. Frankfurt presents the willing addict not as an embarrassment, but as an interesting though paradoxical result of his hierarchical theory. And Gerald Dworkin is also willing to bite hard on this unpalatable bullet:

> . . . a person who wishes to be restricted in various ways, whether by the discipline of the monastery, regimentation of the army, or even by coercion, is not, on that account alone, less autonomous. . . . In my conception, the autonomous person can be a tyrant or a slave, a saint or sinner, a rugged individualist or champion of fraternity, a leader or follower. (Dworkin 1988, 18, 29)

But there are good reasons to be disturbed when profoundly regimented followers—who affirm their subservience—are counted as free and authentic. After all, authenticity claims have served more often as fetters than liberators. This individual has no opportunities nor alternatives; but no matter, happily he is authentically suited for such a blinkered existence, because he is satisfied with his narrow world. This laborer's situation offers no opportunities, no decisions; but fortunately, she prefers and approves such drudgery and does not wish to make decisions and face choices. This woman is wedged tightly between the demands of an intolerant society and a domineering husband; but she is not wronged, since she wills her role as helpmate and is authentically subservient. He is a true ruler, they are satisfied subjects; he is a natural leader, she a natural follower; he is well-suited to manage, and they are authentically docile workers. Of course, contemporary champions of hierarchical authenticity do not defend such abuses,[1] but the point is how easily—and often—"authenticity" is put to such repressive uses.

So how do we deal with the problem of the authentically happy slave? One way is by requiring procedural sophistication in selecting authentic higher-order preferences: one must evaluate rationally and without being under deception. That is the direction that Dworkin travels in his recently revised views on autonomy:

> I now believe that . . . it is not the identification or lack of identification that is crucial to being autonomous, but the capacity to raise the question of whether I will identify with or reject the reasons for which I now act. (1988, 15)

But there are limits to that tack. Unless one is willing to posit Susan Wolf's True and Good, there remains the possibility of someone reflectively recognizing and approving a stifling and subservient role (perhaps because of such a strong and pervasive acculturation process that reflection only affirms the narrow role). The "authentically subservient" wife may know the process that stifled her larger hopes and interests and now be grateful for—and approve of and identify with—that process as essential for renunciation of her now-despised willfulness and independence. Her *reason* for her commitment to subservience is simply that it is right for husbands to have complete authority over wives, and she now identifies with and reflectively approves that reason. We may despise such reasoning and the acculturation that shaped it. But short of granting autonomy exclusively to those who hold their beliefs and commitments for all the right reasons—and that will not only require a True and Good, but will also leave the class of autonomous individuals very exclusive indeed—it is difficult for even the most sophisticated hierarchical view to avoid attributing autonomy and authenticity to the willing addict and satisfied subservient wife. (Of course, there is another way to enrich reason-identification and procedural independence: by requiring that the autonomous individual have real and substantial and continuing opportunities to explore other paths and possibilities. But that makes hierarchical authenticity into *natural* authenticity).

On the natural authenticity model, the paradox of the happy slave is eliminated, and without appeal to obscure or transcendent standards for rational reflection. Natural authenticity involves commitments that function to keep paths and options open when they might otherwise be abandoned and lost (during periods when they yield no immediate advantages). But the happy slave's devotion to servitude is not like that. Rather than enhancing opportunity by keeping a favorite option open, it stifles the slave's range of opportunity by blocking consideration of alternative pathways. And when that is recognized, then there is no temptation to claim that the "happy slave" (whose brutal situation has snuffed out any wish for escape) and the enervated factory worker (who has abandoned hope of richer opportunities) and the subjugated wife (whose stifling environment has killed her dreams of richer options) are authentically docile and subservient and unimaginative. It is true that they now embrace the terrible necessity that drained their capacity to will other opportunities; but they are not "authentic" drudges and slaves. The stifling environment that compels them to trudge down a single narrow path has undermined their authenticity, since their single-minded devotion stifles and con-stricts—rather than enlarges—their options and opportunities. We might just as plausibly—or implausibly—count Seligman's dogs that developed "learned helplessness" (after repeated sub-jection to inescapable shock) as *authentically* passive because they now accept shock without attempting to escape.[2] One who is beaten down to resignedly following a single path because no other can be imagined or desired is not embracing that path in order to maintain an additional long-term option. Such willful single-path submission is a corrupted pseudoauthenticity that fails to fulfill the option-enhancing function of (natural) authen-ticity.

The addiction of the willing addict constricts rather than enlarges options. But in the absence of positive reinforcers along alternative paths, it is not surprising that other options are effectively extinguished as the individual develops an obses-sive attachment to the single path (or theory, or religious enthu-siasm, or role) that has on occasion proved positively reinforc-ing. If that path only occasionally delivers benefits, that will not temper the devotion; to the contrary, such a variable-interval pattern of reinforcement is more likely to entrench the obses-sive attachment. In such cases, we have a dedicated drug addict, a true believer, or a committed cultist. That such per-version of authenticity is possible does not imply that more typ-ical option-enhancing authenticity is less important or less use-ful.

It might be objected that the natural authenticity model lumps dedicated scientists with obsessive cultists: that anyone who makes a deep commitment slides from authenticity into pseudoauthenticity. But the natural authenticity model easily distinguishes the cultist from the committed scientist. The sci-entist is authentically committed when she strongly favors one theoretical line, pursuing it even if it seems less immediately promising. If it becomes an obsession, and blinds her to any other possibilities, then her distorted pseudoauthenticity is counterproductive. When commitment is joined with aware-ness of other open possibilities—possibilities that might be bet-ter than the one pursued—it is a beneficial natural authentic-ity; and one may pursue such a commitment—whether fox, philosopher or scientist—without it becoming a blinding, numbing, option-eliminating obsession. In short, commitments of faith are important for theory-pursuing scientists and duck-pursuing foxes, and faith is "the substance of things hoped for." But faith can be lost in two different ways: in the more common manner of lost hope and extinguished interest (as when Reynard eventually abandons the futile path to Farmer John's); or through transmogrification into obsessive attachment and refusal to consider alternatives or doubts. In the latter case, commitments change from opportunity enhancing to opportunity closing, and from authenticity to its corrupted counterfeit.

### Linking Autonomy with Authenticity

Natural authenticity restores the link between authenticity and autonomy-as-alternatives: an important link that other accounts attempt to sever. Frankfurt, for example, claims that authenticity renders autonomy-as-alternatives superfluous. The willing addict—with no open alternatives—nonetheless acts autonomously through his authentic willing.

Frankfurt's policy makes sense in conditions of triage: mysterious libertarian-choice autonomy cannot survive in our nonmiraculous naturalistic world, so we must save what we can (autonomy-as-authenticity) and abandon what we must (autonomy-as-alternatives), lest we lose all. But the natural authenticity account preserves both authenticity and alternatives and affirms their close and mutually supportive connection.

Autonomy-as-alternatives is the mundane natural process—found in humans, mice and foxes, but not in digger wasps—of exploring alternatives and preserving options. Autonomy-as-alternatives requires no powers of miraculous choice; instead it offers precisely what our changing natural world has shaped us to prefer: not alternatives available only to some mysterious noncontingent transcendent choice, but rather alternatives that are available to us as our environmental conditions change. Natural authenticity is not in opposition to such alternatives-autonomy. To the contrary, natural authenticity maintains and preserves beneficial paths (and friendships and principles and theories) when they might otherwise be lost due to short-term disadvantages.

Understanding how natural authenticity complements autonomy-as-alternatives makes it easier to answer one of Gerald Dworkin's objections. Alternatives are important to both humans and white-footed mice, but autonomy (autonomy-as-alternatives) is not an absolute good. Were the world static, autonomy would be of little use. And even in our changing world, autonomy is not an unmixed benefit. Gerald Dworkin argues that "autonomy that insists upon substantive independence [as does autonomy-as-alternatives] is not one that has a claim to our respect as an ideal," because (in contrast to traditional authenticity) it "makes autonomy inconsistent with loyalty, objectivity, commitment, benevolence, and love" (Dworkin 1988, 21). Dworkin's inconsistency claim is overstated, but even if it were true, it would not show that autonomy is not valuable; rather, it would show that the good of autonomy may sometimes conflict with other goods, including loyalty and love. If I am committed to the care and welfare of my children, I am limited: I cannot pursue the path of artistic abandon, free of all family constraints, on a tropical island. Along similar lines, William Shakespeare writes:

> Let me not to the marriage of true minds
> Admit impediments. Love is not love
> Which alters when it alteration finds, . . .

And there is that quality to some degree in all commitments: commitment to a theory or research program or scientific paradigm is not quite like commitments of love, but it does mean that one will give less attention to—and thus have less readily available—alternatives. As Thomas Kuhn has noted (1962, chap. 6), commitment to a particular "paradigm" may cause one to overlook potentially important phenomena and thus miss the alternatives and discoveries to which they might lead.

But while such commitments may compromise autonomy, that is not an overwhelming problem for autonomy-as-alternatives. In the first place, the fact that autonomy-as-alternatives will not perfectly accommodate every possible good is not a refutation of the view: autonomy remains a very desirable good, even if—in our less than perfect world—it sometimes conflicts with other goods and we cannot have everything. Second, there is no reason to think that autonomy must be the overarching highest good: compromising it for the joys and benefits of love and loyalty may be a very decent compromise. Third, our commitments need not be blinding obsessions. While being, in Yeats' phrase, "deaf and dumb and blind in love" might well close the way to intelligent reflection on other possibilities, there may be somewhat less debilitating commitments. I may, after all, decide that my loyalty and love and trust were misplaced. And for all the power of Kuhn's discussion of paradigm commitments, it does seem possible for some scientists to be aware of flaws and problems in the theories they deeply favor and to consider and even switch to alternative paths. Fourth—and this is where natural authenticity strengthens autonomy-as-alternatives—commitments often open a range of alternatives otherwise unavailable:[3] some social paths may require genuine commitment as the price of admission; and as Kuhn notes, commitment to carrying out the normal science research projects within a particular paradigm may often be the best means of gaining new scientific information and seizing opportunities. But "authentic commitments" not only open new alternatives, they also *keep* alternatives available that might otherwise be forgotten and lost: alternatives such as temporarily less promising research programs, to continue the Kuhn example.

In our natural world—in which change occurs, but typically with order and continuity rather than capriciously—authenticity is a natural complement to autonomy-as-alternatives. The natural authenticity account explains why both alternatives and commitments are desirable and (generally) compatible, and it accomplishes that in a simpler and more parsimonious fashion: by drawing both under the same explanatory principle and fitting authenticity into a natural explanatory setting as an alternative-enhancing partner to autonomy-as-alternatives. The combination of natural authenticity and natural autonomy-as-alternatives may not encompass all possible goods; but by putting solid animal flesh on the bones of the emaciated compatibilist account of "could-have-done-otherwise," naturalized autonomy gives substance and function to genuine alternatives, while avoiding the slide into libertarian mysterious choice.

# 4

---

## Moral Responsibility

The previous chapters have been an attempt to make Darwinian sense of autonomy and authenticity. Rather than separating human powers and privileges from the rest of the natural animal world, the value of both autonomy-as-alternatives and authenticity lies deep in our natural animal history. Autonomy is vitally important to animals that live and learn in a changing and uncertain world. But some will see a gaping hole in this naturalized account of animal autonomy: where is moral responsibility?

That an adequate account of autonomy must support moral responsibility is a philosophical article of faith. C. A. Campbell asserts that the sort of freedom that philosophers must seek to understand is the sort of freedom that supports moral responsibility and just deserts:

> It is not seriously disputable that the kind of freedom in question is the freedom which is commonly recognised to be in some sense a precondition of moral responsibility. Clearly, it is on account of this integral connection with moral responsibility that such exceptional importance has always been felt to attach to the Free Will problem. (Campbell 1957, 159)

And Willard Gaylin regards the connection between autonomy and moral responsibility as so obvious that it need only be noted to be affirmed: "Freedom demands responsibility; autonomy demands culpability." (Gaylin 1983, 338) But how can natural autonomy support moral responsibility?

It cannot. Autonomy is part of the natural world, requiring neither mysteries nor miracles. It is rooted deep in animal behav-

31

ior and existed long before humans. But moral responsibility is different. It cannot be squeezed into a natural autonomy account.[1]

The project of this book is to examine some traditional philosophical doctrines—humans are uniquely autonomous, moral, and morally responsible—and the claims of special human powers that support those distinctive human characteristics and thus distinguish humans from the rest of the natural world. Darwinism does not rule out such radical species uniqueness, but from the Darwinian perspective it is unusual, unexpected, and suspect. The supposed chasm between autonomous humans and all other animals was bridged by tracing autonomy to its shared roots in animal behavior. Without giving away too much of the plot, a similar solution will be proposed when considering morality: humans are moral, but not uniquely so. But moral responsibility requires a different approach to closing the gap between humans and the rest of the animal world: nonhuman animals cannot be morally responsible, and neither can human animals.

Some may see this as a fatal flaw in the proposed account of natural autonomy: Moral responsibility is inseparably linked to autonomy ("autonomy demands culpability"); thus if moral responsibility cannot be encompassed within the naturalized autonomy account, then naturalized autonomy fails.

The inference is legitimate, but the premise is not. It is true that naturalized autonomy cannot support moral responsibility, but the assertion that an adequate account of autonomy must support moral responsibility is open to challenge. That challenge takes us to difficult and probably irresolvable questions of metaphilosophical preference. Three different positions, involving basically different world views, are possible. First, one might prefer to hang onto moral responsibility at all costs, including the costs of mysterious and miraculous human powers of transcendence and creativity. Some take this position reluctantly: moral responsibility cannot be given up, so we must leave room for miracles; the cost is sloppy, nonscientific thought and an end to any hope of achieving an adequate scientific empirical account of our world and ourselves; but no price is too great for saving moral responsibility. Others embrace the position enthusiastically: moral responsibility requires miracles and mysteries, and that gives us a good excuse to preserve a realm of mystery and miracles where science cannot encroach and empirical study threaten, a realm in which humans are special creations separate from and above the grubby natural world. Certainly it is possible to hold such a view, either enthusiastically or regretfully: after all, if one is willing to accept miracles and mysteries, then one can believe anything at all, with no limits imposed by either science or logic.

There is a second possible position: miracles are unacceptable, and any adequate account of behavior (including autonomous behavior) must stay squarely within the natural nonmiraculous world; the naturalized account of autonomy cannot support moral responsibility; moral responsibility is an essential and inseparable part of any adequate account of autonomy; therefore there can be no workable account of autonomy within the naturalist system, and autonomy must be discarded as superstition. This position goes beyond desert landscape empiricism into hair-shirt asceticism and not only precludes examination of our deep-grained notions of autonomy, but also blocks efforts to salvage a workable natural account of autonomy. The previous chapters have attempted to discover the deep natural roots of a demystified autonomy and demonstrate the essential animal foundation of human hierachical enhancements of autonomy. There is no reason to discard genuine natural autonomy because of its unfortunate confusion with the miracle-working version.

A third approach seems the most promising. There is something important in our traditional emphasis on autonomy, and we can integrate those important elements into a workable naturalistic account of autonomy that explains why autonomy is valuable to humans and other animals. But in order to find these deep-rooted naturalistic elements of autonomy, the traditional autonomy account must be pruned back and some of the miraculous nonnatural branches eliminated. We will be left with a cleaner and healthier yet recognizable account of autonomy: an account that explains what is genuinely valuable in autonomy for animals like ourselves and that can be understood and studied in a larger naturalistic framework. What the naturalistic autonomy account keeps is the emphasis on autonomy-as-alternatives, which also makes sense of authenticity. What is lost is autonomy as a foundation for moral responsibility. But when naturalized autonomy is carefully scrutinized, few (except those who mourn the loss of miracles and special human uniqueness, and perhaps some adamant retributivists) will miss moral responsibility.

A major remaining task is to show why naturalized autonomy-as-alternatives cannot support moral responsibility and why that is a virtue rather than a fault. But showing why natural autonomy cannot support moral responsibility immediately raises the question of compatibilism. Three possibilities concerning autonomy and moral responsibility were considered above. First, keep a miraculous autonomy account that supports moral responsibility; second, throw out both moral responsibility and autonomy, since moral responsibility is inseparably linked to autonomy, and moral responsibility cannot be part of the naturalistic system; or third, extract a workable naturalistic account of autonomy, and discard the miracles and mysteries that are required for moral responsibility. But this neglects what most contemporary philosophers would immediately insist is a fourth—and most promising—alternative: compatibilism. On the compatibilist view, autonomy and moral responsibility are *both* compatible with naturalism, and miracles and mysteries are required for neither. So before going on to examine the strengths and advantages of naturalized autonomy *without* moral responsibility, it is first necessary to show why a compatibilist view *cannot* save moral responsibility: that is, why a naturalist account that saves both autonomy and moral responsibility is *not* a workable fourth alternative.

### Why Moral Responsibility Cannot be Naturalized

Compatibilists insist that autonomy and moral responsibility do not require miracles, that autonomy and moral responsibility are *compatible* with the scientific-naturalist world view. They are half-right. Compatibilist accounts of autonomy by contemporary philosophers tend to overemphasize higher rational powers of reflection and deliberation that are uniquely human (an understandable tendency, since most contemporary philosophers are reflective and deliberative and human); and they tend to underestimate or ignore the presence of autonomy among less reflective individuals (including among other species). Nonetheless, compatibilists have made substantial contributions to our understanding of autonomy and have demonstrated that one can be profoundly and reflectively and decisively autonomous without the aid of deities or miracles or mysteries. Contemporary compatibilist accounts of autonomy are not without their problems, and neglect of autonomy among the less reflective is not their only shortcoming. Some of those problems will be discussed later, but overall the compatibilist accounts of autonomy have been helpful and productive steps in the demystifying and naturalizing of autonomy.

The main problems with compatibilist accounts of autonomy are not in the autonomy accounts themselves, but rather in what the compatibilists have thought must *follow* from the establishment of compatibilist autonomy. Having made the natural world safe for autonomy, they have assumed a secure place for moral responsibility as well. That is not a surprising or philosophically unique assumption: autonomy and moral responsibility are generally regarded as inseparable, the presence of one serving as a guarantee of the other. Jane is autonomous, she acts freely, so she must be morally responsible. John is not morally responsible, so he cannot be acting autonomously. Or once again, as Willard Gaylin puts it: "Freedom demands responsibility; autonomy demands culpability" (1983, 338).

Common as this assumption is, it is ungrounded. The establishment of compatibilist autonomy does not establish moral responsibility, and denial of moral responsibility does not entail denial of autonomy. The confusion stems from failing to appreciate how different compatibilist natural autonomy is from the miracle-working libertarian autonomy that traditionally propped up moral responsibility.

Miracle-working libertarian autonomy is designed precisely to save moral responsibility. Indeed, it is so dedicated to the establishment of moral responsibility and just deserts and retribution-justification that it typically saves moral responsibility at the expense of an intelligible account of autonomy. Libertarian autonomous choice has no causal antecedents, does not stem from my own character and history, is not a product of my personality or my character, and is not shaped by the environment that shaped me. It doesn't matter that we have different environmental histories, different educational opportunities, different levels of encouragement and support and success: our miraculous libertarian autonomous choices transcend all differences, and thus we ourselves and nothing else—not the gods who made us, the genes that directed us, nor the environments that shaped us—bear moral responsibility for our choices and their consequences, and we alone deserve the rewards or retribution for our wonderful miraculous transcendent choices. We make ourselves through such choices (as the existentialists assert) rather than choosing from the characters we already have; and thus we are totally responsible for the choices we make and the characters we fashion.

But for the naturalist, frustration rapidly boils over into impolite questions: where does this choice come from, if not from my formed character? If the choice transcends my history and my character and my desires and my intellect, then how can it be *my* choice at all? Such miraculous autonomous choices seem completely detached from me and my choosing and my deliberative processes, all of which have been shaped by my cumulative genetic and learning and social histories. The miraculous saving of moral responsibility thus seems to be at the expense of a coherent account of autonomous choice. But in any case, libertarian miraculous autonomy protects moral responsibility from environmental encroachment: that is, after all, precisely what it was designed to do.

Compatibilist autonomy is a different matter. Compatibilist accounts of my own free choices fail to establish moral responsibility for those choices. That failure is obscured by the traditional assumption of an unbreakable bond between autonomy and moral responsibility. Such a bond may be present for the libertarians, but it is not there for the naturalistic accounts of the compatibilists. Thus the typical compatibilist assumption that establishment of compatibilist autonomy is sufficient for securing compatibilist moral responsibility is unjustified.

Consider, after all, what compatibilist accounts of autonomy really do contribute to our understanding of autonomy. Frankfurt, for example, claims that autonomy stems from higher-order reflection on one's preferences: if one not only wills as one wishes, but also has a will that moves in ways one reflectively and decisively approves, then one enjoys a liberal portion of free will and autonomy. As already noted, such reflective powers are valuable: they enlarge our options by giving us expanded resources for reviewing and selecting paths. But important as that may be as an enhancement of autonomy, it soon crumbles if asked to bear the weight of moral responsibility.

Irene favors generosity, and she reflectively—and decisively—approves of her generous motives. Irene is thus genuinely (authentically) generous, and she has reflective resources for maintaining her generous behavior through considerable stress and in a variety of environments, and those resources enhance her options and possibilities. But her moral responsibility for her generous impulses (and for her reflective capacities and her reflective approval of her generosity) is another matter entirely. She has generous motives, but that she has such motives does not make her morally responsible for them: they are the fortunate product of her generous genes or good upbringing or supportive community, none of which gives grounds for moral responsibility and just deserts. (Of course, some may say she is morally responsible—deserves reward—for her generous impulses simply because she has them, even if it is merely a matter of her good genetic luck. That seems implausible to me. In any case, it is not the view of such sophisticated compatibilists as Frankfurt, for it makes their hierarchical levels of higher-order reflection superfluous.)

What then is the source of compatibilist moral responsibility? Is it Irene's special powers of higher-order reflectiveness? But that is implausible as grounds for moral responsibility, for whether one is reflective or impulsive is likewise a product of one's inclinations and cultural training. Perhaps, then, the moral responsibility is not in the reflective capacities, but in the reflective decision made with those capacities: Irene is morally responsible for her generous acts and generous character because of her reflective—and perhaps decisive—choice and favoring of such acts and character. But what sort of choice is that? It cannot be a libertarian inexplicable choice if this is to remain a naturalist-compatibilist defense of moral responsibility. If the choice is not a miraculous mystery, then we can inquire into the causes and conditions of her higher-order choice. Irene reflectively favors generosity; Julia reflectively rejects generous impulses, opting instead for acquisitiveness. Why does Irene decisively choose one way, Julia the other? For an answer, we shall turn—if we are to remain naturalists—to the conditions that shaped one to deeply and reflectively favor generosity and the other greed. But examining those conditions is not likely to turn up anything that will establish moral responsibility; to the contrary, the more closely we scrutinize such shaping the more rapidly the illusion of moral responsibility disappears. For however decisive and reflective such choices are, they must be rooted in causes and conditions not of Irene's or Julia's making.

Of course, one might then return to the reflective process in search of moral responsibility. Had Julia reflected longer and harder, she also might have come to favor generosity; and it was up to her to make the choice of whether to reflect briefly or profoundly. That option is pursued by Daniel Dennett:

> Finally, the model I propose points to the multiplicity of decisions that encircle our moral decisions and suggests that in many cases our ultimate decision as to which way to act is less important phenomenologically as a contributor to our sense of free will than the prior decision affecting our deliberation process itself: the decision, for instance, not to consider any further, to terminate deliberation; or the decision to ignore certain lines of inquiry. (1978, 297)

Thus we can affirm "our sense of ourselves as responsible free agents" by making a decision to finally "terminate deliberation" and take action, "in the full knowledge that the eventualities may prove that I decided in error, but with the acceptance of responsibility in any case" (297).

Dennett's attempt to base moral responsibility not on the larger processes of deliberation, but instead on limited specific choices (such as the choice to terminate deliberation and act) fits the traditional pattern: make the key choice for which one is morally responsible as small and unobtrusive as possible, so that it will seem to require only the tiniest and least objectionable area of special choice. C. A. Campbell (a miracle-embracing libertarian) bases moral responsibility on narrow decisions to exert or withhold the effort to rise to duty and combat desire (not the effort itself, nor the desire, nor the sense of duty, but merely the choice to make an effort); and Dennett (a naturalist-compatibilist) bases moral responsibility not on the deliberations, nor the acts, nor even on the decision made, but rather on the small and innocent choice to stop deliberating.

It doesn't work. Making the crucial moral-responsibility-preserving choice smaller makes the problem less obvious, but the problem is there, plain and clear, as soon as we focus in carefully. Look hard at this decision to "terminate deliberation." Mary deliberates for a while and then decides "to ignore certain lines of inquiry" and "terminate deliberation" without considering further. Unfortunately, the lines of inquiry she chooses to ignore are of vital importance, and as a result, she makes a poor choice and her acts are destructive. Marguerite, in the same quandary, deliberates long and hard, covers more carefully a wider-ranging inquiry, considers a rich variety of alternatives, and thus makes a wise choice and acts constructively. If their choices to stop or continue deliberation are inexplicable miraculous mysteries, then no further inquiries into their decisions are possible; but if this is to be a naturalistic account, then we must ask why Mary stopped deliberating too quickly, and why Marguerite is such a dedicated and diligent and effective deliberator. Pursuit of those questions swiftly undermines any claim that Mary and Marguerite are morally responsible for their choices to cease or continue deliberations. The capacity and the inclination for careful and prolonged deliberation are learned. Marguerite's deliberative efforts were encouraged and rewarded (her parents delighted in careful thought, and dedicated deliberation was carried out in an environment that rewarded such efforts), and her careful deliberative perseverance was strengthened. Mary's early deliberations were treated impatiently, and thoughtful hesitation typically resulted in lost opportunities and parental reprimands; and Mary did not acquire deliberative strength and endurance. Neither case offers grounds for just deserts and moral responsibility.

No matter how careful or prolonged or hierarchical the deliberation, it cannot support compatibilist moral responsibility. Nonetheless, such deliberation—and decisions about when to stop deliberating—can help to establish that we are "responsible," in at least two important senses of that word. First, if I think carefully before I act, not only deliberating but reflectively considering the extent and adequacy of my deliberations, then I am more likely to "act responsibly": I act with care and caution, after due consideration, rather than acting rashly. But though I may be "responsible" in that sense, such responsibility is not the *moral* responsibility of just deserts. Marguerite is certainly a *responsible* person—she acts carefully and deliberately, she does not make rash decisions—but it is a separate and open question whether she is *morally* responsible (deserving of praise or reward) for being so cautiously and meticulously *responsible*. (Even if one had good reasons—and I know of none—for thinking that the range of morally responsible acts is precisely coextensive with the range of acts done by *responsible* individuals, that would still require proof: "moral responsibility" means something quite different from "being a responsible individual," and the former does not immediately follow from the latter.)

Second, and even more importantly, such careful deliberation contributes to my "responsibility" for and control over my own decisions and choices and life. Through careful reflection I am in a position to "take responsibility" for my choices and acts: I make my own choices, I take responsibility for them, and I do not want my choices either trivialized or thwarted. But that additional important sense of responsibility is again not *moral* responsibility: it is not the sort of responsibility that justifies just deserts, praise and blame, reward and punishment. The responsibility that one can make and take is instead a special kind of role-responsibility, what might be called "take-charge" responsibility because of contemporary emphasis on *taking* responsibility for one's acts and character and life. This take-charge responsibility—the subject of the next chapter—is important and valuable in its own right, but it is also important that it be distinguished from moral responsibility. Many of the contemporary compatibilist arguments that aim to reconcile naturalism with *moral* responsibility miss their mark, instead establishing that *role* or *take-charge* responsibility is compatible with naturalism.

Natural autonomy (autonomy-as-alternatives) does preserve responsibility; but it is *take-charge* responsibility rather than the *moral* responsibility of just deserts and retribution. When those types of responsibility are carefully distinguished, most *naturalists* may agree that *take-charge* responsibility is the baby and *moral* responsibility the bath water.

# 5

Responsibility
and the Self-Made Self

Responsibility has been sought in many places, from the mundane to the miraculous. But recently some philosophers have suggested a bold new basis for responsibility: we make it—and take it—ourselves. Not through miraculous self-choosing, nature-transcending creativity, but by the ordinary process of shaping and approving our characters as we live our day-to-day, this-worldly lives. We are not Prime Movers Unmoved, but we are genuine movers and shakers. We do things, choose things, make things—including ourselves—and take responsibility for what we make.

Self-made-responsibility is prominent in Harry G. Frankfurt's claim that we take responsibility through identification:

> To the extent that a person identifies himself with the springs of his actions, he takes responsibility for those actions and acquires moral responsibility for them; moreover, the question of how the actions and his identifications with their springs is caused is irrelevant to the questions of whether he performs the actions freely or is morally responsible for performing them. (Frankfurt 1975, 122)

Along similar lines, Daniel Dennett emphasizes taking responsibility through self-making:

> I take responsibility for any thing I make and then inflict upon the general public. . . . Common wisdom has it that much the same rationale grounds personal responsibility; I have created and unleashed an agent who is myself; if its acts produce harm, the manufacturer is held responsible. I think this common wisdom is indeed wisdom. . . . (Dennett 1984, 85)

These views have strong appeal: while avoiding mysticism and miracles, they emphasize the possibility and desirability of self-making and of taking responsibility for self. This places responsibility for myself exactly where I want it: in my hands, in my purposes and decisions and efforts, and in no one else's. I can decide for myself what is worthwhile and how to pursue and accomplish it, and such self-making and self-modifying exorcises the spectre of fatalistic futility. If my laziness frustrates me, I am not a passive victim cursed with a fatal flaw: I can, if I wish, change my character, and make—or re-make—myself. In that sense I am responsible for myself, and glad to be so.

Unfortunately, champions of responsibility for self often slide from those legitimate self-responsibility claims to claims concerning *moral* responsibility. Frankfurt treats taking-responsibility-for-self as the very process by which moral responsibility is acquired: when "a person identifies himself with the springs of his actions, he takes responsibility for those actions and acquires moral responsibility for them"; and when Dennett considers a "thoroughly mean-spirited" individual, he suggests that since "one can be as responsible for one's character as for any other artifact arising from one's past efforts," therefore this despicable individual indeed may be one "who deserves to be despised" (Dennett 1984, 167). Thus the route from responsibility-for-self-making to moral responsibility seems smooth and swift. But in fact there are formidable obstacles along the path from responsibility-for-self-making to moral (just-deserts) responsibility: obstacles—it will be argued—that make the path impassable.

I am responsible for my own life, I can make my own choices, I take responsibility for myself. These are high-sounding sentiments, but there is nothing mysterious or esoteric about them. Such responsibility for self falls into the same category as most of the workaday responsibilities that we (as responsible individuals) exercise. I am responsible for preparing my courses, keeping the minutes of the budget committee, picking up my child from school. These are my responsibilities, and I shall legitimately take offense at any suggestion that I am not responsible or that I am incapable of handling such responsibilities. But however much I may value and claim and take such responsibilities, they do not imply moral (just-deserts) responsibility.

When we look closely at my responsibility for my job, my children, my offices—and for myself—it is obvious that that responsibility is distinct and different from moral responsibility. Moral responsibility is fundamentally related to fairness, to justice, to just deserts. If I am morally responsible for the theft, then it is fair and just that I be punished for it; and I can be justly blamed and justly punished (or justly praised and justly rewarded) only when I am morally responsible. But the responsibilities discussed above—responsibility for an office, a job, a role, a task—fall under a different rubric. H. L. A. Hart (1968, 212) characterizes the responsibilities of offices and jobs as role-responsibility; to highlight the elements emphasized by Frankfurt and Dennett, a somewhat broader category—including responsibility for roles as well as for self—might be called take-charge-responsibility (TCR) and distinguished from moral or just-deserts-responsibility (JDR). TCR is important; indeed, its importance could hardly be overstated. But it is not grounds for moral responsibility: it is not JDR, and it provides no justification for ascriptions of JDR.

Consider my role as secretary for the budget committee. I take responsibility for the role, I acknowledge that responsibility, I have full take-charge-responsibility. But that TCR does not imply just-deserts-responsibility. For it is perfectly consistent and understandable to say: Bruce is responsible—fully responsible—for keeping the records of the committee; but he should not be blamed for failing at it (because his senility or psychoses or family difficulties make it impossible for him to effectively carry out his duties). Thus one may have full TCR without JDR. One may be role-responsible but not morally responsible for the manner in which one discharges that role. TCR and JDR are distinct and different species.

The same point can be seen from the other direction. I may have full TCR for the role of secretary but have no JDR for carrying out the tasks splendidly. I have an excellent assistant who does all the work (so I deserve no credit), or I am doing a task far below my capacities in order to shirk tasks better suited to my outstanding abilities, or my superb secretarial abilities are merely the lucky result of my genetics (I am blessed with the committee secretary gene) and I have done nothing to enhance or strengthen or sustain that God-given gift. (Even if I did make efforts to improve my abilities those efforts cannot establish my moral responsibility; but that claim is not being argued here.[1]

The immediate point is only that TCR clearly can exist without JDR.) So again, I may be fully TCR while deserving no praise, while being devoid of JDR.

The TCR/JDR distinction is also seen by looking at the ways in which one can actually take responsibility. I can take responsibility—take-charge-responsibility—for the role of committee secretary (I can volunteer for the job, or just take on the task when no one else does it); but I cannot simply take responsibility (JDR) when praise and blame and just deserts are at stake. If someone questions whether I deserve praise for splendidly carrying out the role of committee secretary ("Bruce deserves no credit; his assistant did all the work"; or "Bruce deserves no praise; he was just lucky enough to have the right genes for the job"), I cannot dismiss such questions by *taking* responsibility. Nor can I take responsibility for failing to do the task, when the question is whether I am JDR for the failure (because of my psychosis). My wish to take moral responsibility for my failure may be touching, but it will carry no weight in actually establishing JDR.

### Take-Charge-Responsibility for Self

Nothing changes when the the take-charge-responsibility is for myself. TCR for one's own self is supremely important, but it is not moral (just-deserts) responsibility. Certainly it is my responsibility to consider the values I hold and the sort of person I am and wish to be. I may seek advice and consider criticisms, but I have responsibility for myself and I—not my parents, my party, nor my therapist—will make the decisions. If I am denied that responsibility (if someone else has take-charge-responsibility for me), then I suffer important and demeaning and even depersonifying[2] loss. But brief examination of how self-making skills develop shows that my strong take-charge-responsibility for myself does not imply just-deserts-responsibility.

There are important skills and strengths that enhance effective self-making: knowledge of viable options, imagination and inquisitiveness to discover a wide variety of possibilities, confidence and courage to make choices and try new paths, fortitude to steadfastly pursue goals. Examining these self-making skills quickly casts doubt on just-deserts-responsibility for self-making, for there is no reason to believe that one is any more morally responsible for self-making skills than for cabinet-making or candle-making or committee-secretary skills.

We know a great deal about how one develops skills of imagination, self-confidence, and fortitude, and also how one fails to develop them. Fortitude is nurtured by early experience of progressively more demanding tasks that can be successfully accomplished by gradually increasing effort. The experience of impossibly difficult tasks—with consequent failed efforts—engenders lethargy. The child whose imaginative quests are supported with delight and encouragement and reassurance learns to explore options and keep an open mind; the child whose explorations are punished, or stifled by subtle parental threats of affection withdrawal, develops a stunted capacity for the vital self-making skills of open exploration. One might quibble about the details of the above psychological accounts, but the point is simply that when the sources of self-making (role-responsibility-taking) skills are soberly examined, it is obvious that the energetic (or lethargic) and imaginative (or dull) individual is not morally responsible for those essential skills, nor for the levels of such skills. Of course, one may take take-charge-responsibility for developing a self with better self-development skills; but no one is just-deserts-responsible for having (or lacking) the capacities to take and effectively exercise take-charge-responsibility for strengthening self-development skills. And to assert (correctly) that the individual may nonetheless have full role (take-charge) responsibility for evaluating and improving such self-making skills merely makes one more turn around the loop: it does not establish just-deserts-responsibility.

When the take-responsibility-for-self arguments of Frankfurt and Dennett are reinterpreted as arguments for TCR (rather than JDR), the weakest points of their arguments are transformed into strengths. Consider Dennett's claim that we all end up roughly equal in our capacities for responsibility:

> . . . moral development is not a race at all, with a single winner and everyone else ranked behind, but a process that apparently brings people sooner or later to a sort of plateau of development. . . . But everyone comes out more or less in the same league. When people are deemed "good enough" their moral education is over, and except for those who are singled out as defective—retarded or psychopathic, for instance—the citizenry

is held to be composed of individuals of roughly equivalent talents, insofar as the demands of citizenship are concerned. Both initial differences and variations in subsequent luck are commonly held to average out. (Dennett 1984, 96)

If this is an argument for moral responsibility (just deserts) based on rough equivalence in skills and capacities, then the flaws in the argument are conspicuous. When we consider capacities for avoiding bad conduct, it is clear that not everyone has "roughly equivalent talents"; and that is even more obvious when the focus is on capacities for positive achievement. Even excluding the "retarded or psychopathic," we remain vastly different in intelligence, education, fortitude, imagination, inquisitiveness, and sympathy. "Initial differences and variations in subsequent luck" do not "average out," but instead are more likely to have cumulative effects. As an obvious example, the initially more skillful player gets more playing time, builds greater stamina, and improves her athletic skills while developing the poise and savvy of the practiced athlete; and the initial small gap (between players who play more and those who play less) widens. We are not roughly equal in opportunities and capacities, and it is both implausible and unfair to base *moral* responsibility judgments on that false assumption.

But if Dennett's "plateau of development" is instead the minimum competency required to exercise *take-charge-responsibility* for self (not to establish just-deserts-responsibility), then it becomes both plausible and generous. Freedom is maximized by treating everyone—except the severely defective—as occupying the same take-charge-responsibility-for-self plateau. Whether one is a master craftsperson or a minimally competent bumbler at self-making, one may legitimately claim and take and exercise a full measure of take-charge-responsibility for self. I am not as skilled at self-making as is my friend Joyce (she has greater intelligence, imagination, and perseverance) but I insist—rightly and reasonably—on taking and exercising equal TCR for myself and on full rights to mold myself as I see fit. But it is something quite different to suggest that because I have minimum-level self-making capacity (which justifies full TCR for myself), I therefore have equal (or any) just-deserts-responsibility for doing well or ill at exercising my equal take-charge-responsibility for myself.

The same point applies to Frankfurt's brusque dismissal of causal history:

> To the extent that a person identifies himself with the springs of his actions, he takes responsibility for those actions and acquires moral responsibility for them; moreover, the question of how the actions and his identifications with their springs is caused is irrelevant to the questions of whether he performs the actions freely or is morally responsible for performing them. (Frankfurt 1975, 122)

But if the issue is moral responsibility and just deserts then causal history *is* relevant. Suppose that Scrooge's deprived and brutal childhood shaped his profound fear of vulnerability and rejection and causes him to approve and identify with his avarice. It is more callous than plausible to suggest that Scrooge's unfortunate history has no bearing on his moral responsibility for his commitment to greed. But if the question is instead whether Scrooge should be able to fully take-responsibility-for-self and pursue the goals he does favor—whatever their causal origins, and whatever the developmental history of his (strong or barely minimal) self-making capacities—that is another matter. Scrooge's causal history results in unfortunate goals and choices and commitments, and acquaintance with that history casts doubt on his moral responsibility for being such a poor practitioner of self-making; but so long as he somehow developed minimally adequate self-making capacities, then (assuming we value freedom above compulsory moral perfectionism) his unfortunate history cannot justify denying Scrooge take-charge responsibility for shaping and living his life as he chooses.

This last point is of the first importance. Denial of moral responsibility is often treated as equivalent to the denial of all individual rights and responsibilities, and thus is thought to open the door to the most brutal and repressive methods of shaping character and controlling behavior. When it is recognized that what is denied is moral responsibilty (JDR) and not role-responsibility-for-self (TCR), it is clear that denial of moral responsibility is not a threat to individual rights. We want the right to follow our own paths, to engage in our own self-making; and that right is fully protected by respect for take-charge-responsibility-for-self. So denial of spurious JDR does not threaten the genuinely valuable TCR, nor the individual rights (such as rights to noninterference) it supports. To the contrary, clear focus on TCR skills (without the fog of moral responsibility) offers new opportunities to nurture and enhance autonomous self-making capacities. In sum, the take-responsibility arguments of Frankfurt and Dennett are better construed as cogent arguments for TCR rather than as implausible arguments for JDR. When that distinction is recognized, we may conclude that TCR is what we really wanted all along.

But is take-charge-responsibility what is wanted by a Darwinian account that is attempting to close the gaps between humans and the rest of the natural world? After all, isn't take-charge-responsibility uniquely human, just as moral responsibility is supposed to be?

No. TCR is an important element of autonomy, but autonomy—as argued in earlier chapters—is not uniquely human. Other animals can and do have role (take-charge) responsibility. Humans may have more elaborate roles and more sophisticated ways of exercising TCR. As noted earlier, human intelligence offers special adaptations for enhancing autonomy. But that is a difference in degree, not a difference in kind that separates humans from the rest of the natural world.

Consider a case of role (take charge) responsibility among nonhumans. In the chimpanzee colony of the Arnhem Zoo (studied extensively by Frans de Waal), there is a very important chimpanzee known as Mama. De Waal describes her thus:

> Mama enjoys enormous respect in the community. Her central position is comparable to that of a grandmother in a Spanish or Chinese family. When tensions in the group reach their peak, the combatants always turn to her—even the adult males. Many a time I have seen a major conflict between two males end up in her arms. Instead of resorting to physical violence at the climax of their confrontation, the rivals run to Mama, screaming loudly. (de Waal 1982, 56)

Thus de Waal finds it quite natural to discuss specific examples of "her reconciliatory role" in the chimpanzee society. That is Mama's responsibility: her role responsibility, her TCR. But not, of course, her moral responsibility. Mama deserves no credit for her reconciliatory successes, and no blame when her reconciliatory powers are overmatched by aggressive conflicts. Still, Mama does have important take-charge responsibilities for peace-keeping, just as other animals have take-charge responsibilities for leading the troop to feeding areas, protecting the young from predators, or supporting a power coalition that keeps order in the community.

Mama and many other nonhuman animals may also have take-charge responsibility for *self*. Mama may not have the take-charge capacities that most humans enjoy, but she may nonetheless have quite enough such powers that interference in her life would be more harmful than beneficial—since compromise of her TCR and her (limited but important) autonomy would be a greater harm than any benefit that might be derived from such interference. Humans typically have better resources for *improving* their TCR, but other animals also sometimes get better (through practice and experience) at their TCR for their roles and tasks and selves. Nonhuman animals are unlikely to deliberately adopt policies and plans for strengthening their TCR; but then, neither do most humans. For both human and nonhuman animals, few of the improvements in TCR are the result of careful deliberative planning.

There will be more discussion of the justification for such noninterference (when paternalism is examined). But before leaving the topic of (limited but significant) TCR for nonhuman animals, it should be noted that this approach may be helpful in explaining why recognition of the rights of other animals (and moral obligations to consider the welfare of nonhuman animals) need *not* imply that humans must constantly interfere with their lives. For if nonhuman animals enjoy some degree of autonomy and TCR, then interference which undermines that autonomy may be a greater harm than the harm prevented by the interference. You may be better at running my life than I am; that does not justify your interference in my life, whether I am human or chimpanzee or wildebeest.

In sum, then, we humans generally have take-charge responsibility; but in that, we are not unique. None of us, whatever our species, have moral responsibility; but with take-charge responsibility, few of us will miss it.

# 6

---

## Virtue, Vice,
## and Moral Responsibility

The preceding chapters have championed a naturalist-Darwinist account of autonomy that celebrates open paths and "take-charge" responsibility—but denies moral responsibility. The remainder of the book will examine the moral view implied by this perspective. But for most philosophers there will be nothing left to discuss: there can be no morality without moral responsibility.

Could morality exist without moral responsibility? In rare philosophical consensus, the answer is no. Peter van Inwagen states the necessary link between moral evaluation and moral responsibility in an offhand and—so he assumes—transparently conclusive example:

> I have listened to philosophers who deny the existence of moral responsibility. I cannot take them seriously. I know a philosopher who has written a paper in which he denies the reality of moral responsibility. And yet this same philosopher, when certain of his books were stolen, said, "That was a *shoddy* thing to do!" But no one can consistently say that a certain act was a shoddy thing to do *and* say that its agent was not morally responsible when he performed it. (1983, 207)

C. A. Campbell (1957) expressed the point even more dramatically: without justly deserved praise and blame one must relinquish "the reality of the moral life." F. C. Copleston claimed that if there were no moral responsibility, then "there would be no objective moral distinction between the emperor Nero and St. Francis of Assisi" (1965, 488). Susan Wolf asserts that without moral responsibility we must:

> . . . stop thinking in terms of what ought and ought not to be. We would have to stop thinking in terms that would allow the possibility that some lives and projects are better than others. (1981, 4)

And Jeffrie Murphy cautions against extending the natural lottery argument too far, since the baleful result would be:

> . . . the end of moral responsibility and the moral significance of human beings that is founded upon such responsibility— would, indeed, spell the end of one's own moral significance. (1988, 400)

But this philosophical consensus is mistaken.[1] Contrary to common philosophical assumption, rich moral lives and substantive moral judgments can flourish without moral responsibility: Esau may be vicious and Jacob virtuous though neither justly deserves blame or praise, reward or punishment.[2]

### Morality and Take-Charge Responsibility

The doctrine that denial of moral responsibility entails denial of morality is based, first, on the confusion discussed in the previous chapter: between take-charge responsibility (TCR) and moral or just-deserts responsibility (JDR). Denial of TCR would indeed undermine morality; denial of JDR does not.

Daniel Dennett emphasizes the importance of take-charge responsibility even as he confuses it with *moral* responsibility:

> We want to be in control of ourselves, and not under the control of others. We want to be agents, capable of initiating, and taking responsibility for, projects and deeds. (1984, 169)

Certainly we want to take responsibility for our projects and our deeds and our moral lives. Without that responsibility our moral lives would be thin indeed, and virtue and vice could not sink their roots in such shallow soil. But that is not the taking of *moral* responsibility. Moral responsibility is the responsibility that supports just deserts and provides a fairness foundation for differential rewards and punishments. The *take-charge* responsibility one *takes* is something else entirely.

Look again at the distinction between moral responsibility

and take-charge responsibility. Albert is responsible for keeping the department records. Perhaps he was assigned that responsibility and merely acquiesced; or possibly he claimed the responsibility for himself, *taking* responsibility for the task. In any case, it is Albert's role and his *role* (his take-charge) responsibility. But his moral responsibility is a separate issue. We can consistently and plausibly maintain that Albert is take-charge responsible for record keeping, while denying his moral responsibility—denying that he deserves praise or condemnation, reward or punishment, or any just deserts whatsoever—for his success or failure in that role. "Albert has taken responsibility for the records; but he is suffering from Alzheimer's, and it would be wrong to blame him (hold him morally responsible) for the terrible mess he has made." Nor is this merely avoiding blame. It applies equally to deserving praise or reward: "Alice did a wonderful job in her role, but she is lucky to have a background that nurtured her excellent organizational skills and steady perseverance; she deserves no credit for her fortunate history and its good results." One might dispute the denial of Alice's or Albert's moral responsibility; but the point here is that establishing take-charge responsibility will leave the moral responsibility question open. Thus take-charge responsibility is *not* moral responsibility, and the denial of moral responsibility does not deny or threaten take-charge responsibility.

The same applies to responsibility for character and moral commitments and moral life. Consider Carol and Elaine, both of whom consider and choose their own moral commitments. Both fiercely resent efforts to deny them the status of moral actors, the right to make their own moral choices. Both affirm: "I decide for myself what is right or wrong, what paths to follow and what moral code to honor. No one makes that decision for me. I take responsibility for my own moral choices and for the development of my own moral character." And indeed they do make their own choices, weighing the teachings of priests and prophets, philosophers and parents, and then deciding for themselves. Thus they have responsibility for their own *moral* lives and characters. In that narrow sense, they have—and take—"*moral* responsibility." But that is not moral responsibility in the sense that justifies just deserts and praise and condemnation. Rather, it is role or *take-charge* responsibility for one's *moral* life.

When people insist that they can and do "take responsibility" for themselves and their acts and their characters, they are typically asserting take-charge responsibility—but it is often confused with *moral* responsibility (even by those who *take* the responsibility). Both Carol and Elaine take and practice take-charge responsibility for their moral lives. But Carol develops a good and virtuous moral life, while Elaine's (perhaps by her own admission) is a failure. No doubt she made, to a significant degree, her own moral bed. It is a separate question whether she deserves to lie in it. When we examine why Carol and Elaine played their moral self-development roles so differently, we discover causal factors that were their good or bad fortune and not ultimately of their own making: perhaps differences in childhood training or early role models, differing capacities for deliberation or imaginative sympathy, or even differing resources for self-control and perseverance. Of course Carol's admirable powers of self-control and sympathy and deliberation (and Elaine's unfortunate weakness and selfishness and flightiness) may be substantially the result of their own choices and activities, and nothing is suggested to disparage the importance of such activities. But that merely pushes the inquiries a step further back: why did Carol strengthen her deliberative and self-control capacities while Elaine became weaker and more dissipated? And thus we push back to causal factors that are the result of good or bad fortune, and not something for which either Carol or Elaine justly deserve reward or punishment.

Someone may insist (implausibly, by my lights) that having take-charge responsibility for moral character and choices is sufficient for moral responsibility. The present point is only that denial or affirmation of *moral* responsibility is a separate and distinct issue from denial or affirmation of *take-charge* responsibility for one's moral life. Therefore it is possible to deny moral responsibility (just deserts responsibility) without denying the importance and legitimacy of taking charge of one's own moral choices and character. And that is all that is required to establish that denial of moral responsibility is not the denial of substantive morality. At the very least, one who claims that loss of real morality must follow from denial of moral responsibility needs an intervening argument to show why denial of *moral* responsibility would make take-charge responsibility for morality impossible. No such argument has been given, and the example of Carol—who practices a rich take-charge responsibility for her moral life, but whose moral responsibility and just deserts remain at least doubtful—indicates that no such argument is likely to be forthcoming. In sum, the loss of take-charge responsibility would do deep damage to morality; in contrast, expurgating moral responsibility purges morality of a burdensome weight of unfairness and obscurity.

Consideration of reflective, deliberative, imaginative, self-controlled Carol—who has *take-charge* but not *moral* responsibility—should also eliminate another confusion about moral responsibility and its supposed necessity for morality. Moral responsibility is often regarded as inseparably linked to free will and autonomy. Harry Frankfurt treats "the questions of whether he performs the actions freely or is morally responsible for performing them" (1975, 122) as so closely joined that they must have the same answer. C. A. Campbell asserts that it is only because of ". . . this integral connection with moral responsibility that such exceptional importance has always been felt to attach to the Free Will problem." (1975, 159). And as noted earlier, Willard Gaylin regards the connection as so obvious that it need only be affirmed to be accepted: "Freedom demands responsibility; autonomy demands culpability." (1983, 338) And since autonomy seems to be essential for morality, it would follow that moral responsibility must also be required. But close attention to Carol helps break the autonomy-moral responsibility link.

Carol has all that most of us would wish for in the way of autonomy: she has opportunities to pursue genuine alternatives, she makes commitments and honors them, she is reflective and knowledgable and self-controlled, and she takes control of her own life and choices and values. Of course she did not make herself from scratch, nor do her choices miraculously transcend her environmental history. Carol—and her rich exercise of autonomy—can live without such powers. But as noted in the discussion of Carol's take-charge responsibility, there are good reasons to question Carol's *moral* (just deserts) responsibility. One may or may not agree that Carol lacks moral responsibility: it is enough that there can be a genuine *question* of whether autonomous take-charge responsible Carol is morally responsible. That question is sufficient to mark the distinction between autonomy and moral responsibility, and it places the burden of proof on those claiming that denial of moral responsibility entails denial of autonomy and thus the denial of morality. Morality may require autonomy; it does not follow that morality requires moral responsibility.

## Moral Behavior without Moral Responsibility

Denying moral responsibility denies neither autonomy nor take-charge responsibility. With that in mind, it is easy to clear up another basic confusion that underlies the common doctrine of no-morality-without-moral-responsibility: confusion concerning *why* moral responsibility is denied. If we start from a setting in which moral responsibility is commonly assumed, then exceptions are based on individual defects. Thus Joseph is not morally responsible for his crime because it did not really come from him: he was not himself, since he was under strain and stress. Joline does not deserve blame because she was compelled or addicted, insane or deceived. *Exceptions* to moral responsibility typically require impairments. Generalizing from such individual defect-based exceptions, it appears that the denial of *all* moral responsibility must undermine *all* claims of competent authorship for actions and thus also undermine the practice and judgment of virtue and vice.

That basic generalization—denying moral responsibility in specific cases is based on impairment, so the *universal* denial of moral responsibility must be based on claims of *universal* impairment—is very tempting, as evidenced by its frequency. C. S. Lewis claims that being denied moral responsibility and just deserts means being treated as so severely defective that one is cast out of the human community. It is to be classified:

> . . . on a level with those who have not yet reached the age of reason or those who never will; to be classed with infants, imbeciles, and domestic animals. But to be punished, however severely, because we 'ought to have known better,' is to be treated as a human person made in God's image. (Lewis 1970)

And P. F. Strawson slips into the same faulty generalization. Strawson claims that denying moral responsibility leads to taking the "objective" attitude toward the individual, treating him as someone who cannot be reasoned with but only handled or cured:

> Seeing someone, then, as warped or deranged or compulsive in behaviour or peculiarly unfortunate in his formative circumstances—seeing someone so tends, at least to some extent, to set him apart from normal participant reactive attitudes on the part of one who so sees him, tends to promote, at least in the civilized, objective attitudes. (Strawson 1974, 9)

And setting *everyone* "apart from normal participant reactive attitudes" of blame and retribution implies that everyone is an incompetent, fit only for our "objective attitudes." Thus universal denial of moral responsibility categorizes everyone as "warped or deranged or compulsive," as infant or imbecile.[3]

From that premised generalization—denial of all moral responsibility entails denial of all competence—the demise of morality follows swiftly. The imbecilic, the deranged, and the compulsive may behave beneficially or detrimentally; but their moral behavior, while perhaps not eliminated, is certainly circumscribed: they cannot act with full virtue or vice, since their capacities for deliberate acts (acts that stem from their developed characters and deliberative judgments) are severely impaired.[4] But this threat to morality comes *not* from denial of moral responsibility. Morality is undermined by the supposed *grounds* for the denial of moral responsibility: namely, universal defect that places everyone in the category of compulsive or imbecile or infant. But the *universal* denial of moral responsibility is not based on denial of cognitive capacities or deliberative powers and certainly is not based on the claim that everyone is defective.

Or rather, the universal denial of moral responsibility *should* not be based on claims of universal defect. Unfortunately, some of the most famous denials of moral responsibility have been. John Hospers' (1958) campaign against moral responsibility is based on what might be called "excuse extensionism": find the excusing conditions that count (in special cases) against moral responsibility and then enlarge and expand those conditions until they apply to everyone always. Hospers starts from a few instances of compulsive unconscious motivation and eventually expands that coercive unconscious control to all significant[5] human behavior.[6] The problem with such excuse-extensionism is that it invites Sidney Hook's response:

> . . . one feels lessened as a human being if one's actions are always excused or explained away on the ground that despite appearances one is really not responsible for them. It means being treated like an object, an infant, or someone out of his mind. (1958, 189).

So it is not surprising that the excuse-extensionist denial of moral responsibility conjures up the spectre of substituting coercive therapy for retribution.[7] Such objections and fears strike telling blows against the excuse-extensionist denial of moral responsibility that rejects responsibility everywhere by finding fault in everyone.

But excuse-extensionism is not the right grounds for total rejection of moral responsibility. Moral responsibility must be cut off at its metaphysical roots, before the question of excuses arises. Moral responsibility is not something that *could* work if only we found the right environment, liberated ourselves from unconscious coercive desires, and carried out rational deliberations free of bias and fallacy. Rather, moral responsibility cannot be integrated consistently into our natural scientific world view.[8] Moral responsibility is the stuff of mysteries and miracles, requiring special acts of uncaused causality and miraculous creativity.[9] All excuses aside, the character and capacities and judgments of even the most rational and deliberative and self-controlled individual are ultimately the product of forces that were not under that individual's control. Compare an individual who is deeply virtuous with another who is profoundly vicious: if we search far enough we shall discover differences in their backgrounds and histories and abilities (differences of fortune that were not of their making) that shaped their characters and capacities. Those differences undermine claims or ascriptions of just deserts and moral responsibility.

This may or may not be an adequate refutation of moral responsibility, but that is not the issue here. The point is that this denial of moral responsibility applies to everyone, including the most profoundly deliberative and self-controlled: it does not base the universal denial of moral responsibility on universal defect. Whatever one thinks of these reasons for denying moral responsibility, they do not deny deliberation and deep character formation and acting from one's own formed and reflectively approved character; thus they do not undermine morality and moral reflection.[10]

## Moral Language Without Moral Responsibility

There is no moral responsibility, but what remains are competent, autonomous individuals who have take-charge responsibility for their acts and lives. There also remains, however, one last source of the no-morality-without-moral-responsibility confusion: the dusty old dictum that "ought implies can."

"Jack and Jill ought to feed their children; but because of terrible drought, they cannot do so." It sounds strange to suggest that Jack and Jill ought to feed their children, though there is no food to be had by any means. It is more natural to say that Jack and Jill ought to *try* to feed their children; and if they do not try, then they are morally bad. But—given the reasons offered earlier for denying *all* moral responsibility—if they do not try, then they *could not* try. (Of course they could try if they tried, but that doesn't take us very far. And they could try if they had different environmental and learning histories, but that doesn't take us any further.) Whether one tries and how hard and at what projects is the product of learning histories and early environments and genetic endowments, and close examination of those sources undermines any claims that Jack and Jill are morally responsible for their striving. (For immediate purposes, one need not agree with that rejection of moral responsibility. The question here is whether one who *does* accept it can also make *moral* and *ought* assertions.) But if one's degree of effort is ultimately the product of environmental influences beyond one's control, then there appears to be no difference between the failure to feed one's children because of harsh drought and the failure to feed one's children from lack of interest or effort. And thus if we cannot say that Jack and Jill ought to feed their children under drought conditions (when no food is available), then apparently neither can we say that they ought to feed their children when they could do so if only they would make the effort. Apparently, then, denial of moral responsibility undercuts ought language and thus severely constricts morality.

This dire result does not follow. Jack and Jill are morally responsible for neither drought nor lethargy, but there remain morally significant differences between the two situations: differences that make it reasonable to use ought language in the latter case, but not in the former. And these differences show how moral ought language can continue to be meaningful and useful in the absence of moral responsibility.

The first difference is that in the drought case, telling Jack and Jill that they ought to feed their children will be useless. Reminding them of their obligations will neither alter the drought conditions nor increase the likelihood that they will feed their children. They already long to feed their children: it is not in their power to do so. But telling *lethargic* Jack and Jill (who are not drought stricken) that they ought to feed their children has at least some possibility of good effect. "You ought to shake off your lethargy, gird your loins, pull up your socks, and feed your children." The effects of such admonitions should not be exaggerated: it will require more than verbal suggestion to reshape the character and behavior of lethargic Jack and Jill. Still, such social pressure and verbal prompting does have some effect in shaping human behavior. Whether locked in lethargy or famine, Jack and Jill are not morally responsible for their failure to feed their children. But changing their social and verbal environment may be one means of modifying their lethargic behavior, while no silver-tongued oratory or heartfelt admonition can have any effect on the drought. Thus ought language is useful when dealing with lethargy (and other vices), and the absence of moral responsibility does not diminish its usefulness.

There is a second and more basic reason why ought language is appropriate when dealing with lethargic Jack and Jill, but not with the Jack and Jill trapped in drought. Jack and Jill suffer through a terrible drought that makes it impossible for them to feed their children, but that is no reflection on their moral character. They have failed in their obligations but through no fault of their own, and they may be as morally upright as are parents who successfully nurture their children. Lethargic Jack and Jill are different. Their failure to feed their children can be traced to their own moral failure: their lack of care and concern for their children, or their selfish and profligate ways, or their deep lethargy. One who makes no effort to care for his or her children is morally corrupt. And since ought claims generally carry some degree of moral approval or disapproval—she did as she ought to, despite the adversity; he ought to have helped, but he neglected to do so—they are appropriate when applied to lethargic and morally deficient Jack and Jill, but not when dealing with the drought victims.

This last point should not be misunderstood. Lethargic Jack and Jill are not morally responsible for their bad characters, and they deserve no blame for their moral shortcomings. They are, nonetheless, morally deficient. Indeed, they may be thoroughly scurrilous moral scum. And that may be worth noting, even though there is no question of blaming them for their bad characters. (After all, if we wish to remedy the situation we shall have to proceed quite differently in dealing with lethargic Jack and Jill than with their drought-stricken namesakes. And we may still hold drought-stricken Jack and Jill up as moral exemplars, who provide positive moral examples for our youth; we shall certainly not encourage our children to emulate the lethargic and morally corrupt couple. So the difference remains important—and morally important—in the absence of just deserts and moral responsibility.)

Of course one could build so much into an "ought" that it would analytically imply moral responsibility. But the point here is that we have an ordinary functional use of "ought" without such a moral responsibility implication, and that is all the argument requires. The claim is not that there is no conceivable moral system that requires moral responsibility, but only that there *is* a workable and adequate moral perspective (the Darwinian perspective that will be further elaborated in the following chapters, for example) that does *not* require moral responsibility.

In the course of arguing that "ought" language can function *without* moral responsibility, it was suggested that lethargic Jack and Jill (who are *not* morally responsible) may be—and be evaluated as—morally scurrilous. That claim will hardly go unchallenged. The opposition is expressed in the earlier quotation from van Inwagen: "No one can consistently say that a certain act was a shoddy thing to do *and* say that its agent was not morally responsible when he performed it."(1983, 207) Van Inwagen's claim is that use of morally evaluative language requires ascription of moral responsibility, and therefore the price of denying moral responsibility is the loss of such basic and essential moral evaluations as "praiseworthy," "blameworthy," "shoddy," "admirable," and "despicable." Daniel Dennett takes this view in his response to the claim that it is "unfair" that we despise the thoroughly mean-spirited individual:

> The retort suggests itself: Who more deserves to be despised than someone utterly despicable. (Dennett 1984, 167)

Mary Midgley espouses the same position:

> Praise and blame are unavoidable forms of moral light and shadow. Without them, the world would appear as a uniform grey. Depression sometimes does confront people with such a

world, when they have ceased to care about anything that happens around them. But this can scarcely be seen as an ideal. (1989, 171)

But universal denial of the justified desert of praise and blame does not paint the world a depressingly uniform moral grey. Or rather it does not paint such a drab scene *unless* one supposes that praise and blame are essentially and inseparably linked to moral evaluation: that to make a moral evaluation, a judgment of virtue or vice, is necessarily to conclude that one justly deserves praise or condemnation; and thus that to deny just deserts entails denial of moral judgments. That supposition, plausible as it may sound, is false. It is false that "someone utterly despicable" therefore "deserves to be despised," and false that a "shoddy" or scurrilous act requires a morally responsible actor. The falsity will be plain if we mark the distinction between *warranting* and *deserving* praise or blame.

It is perfectly consistent to assert that an individual is shallow and selfish—undeniably a moral evaluation—without believing that the person is *deserving* of condemnation. This thoroughly mean-spirited individual is the unfortunate product of a brutal childhood: a childhood that rendered him profoundly and willfully vicious, and would have done the same to each of us had we shared his early misfortune. We conclude that we were lucky, and he was not, and that it is unfair and unjust to blame him for being so vile. But that is not to deny that he really is vile and vicious. He is, in the ambiguous word, despicable. We might well say that he warrants such an evaluation, that he is correctly described as vicious and despicable. But there remains a separate question, requiring a further and distinct argument: He really is vicious; does he deserve blame for being so?

Jacob is profoundly kind and generous. He feels genuine affection for his fellows, and his heartfelt commitment to generosity is confirmed by his reflective higher-order dedication to generosity and kindness as a life he approves and strives to sustain. Merely to state such facts about Jacob is to make a positive moral evaluation of him. Such an evaluation is justified: it is warranted by his morally good character and virtuous acts. But the step from *warranted* positive moral evaluation to justly *deserved* praise (in the sense of it being fair and just that Jacob receive special verbal reward) is actually a long jump: a leap that is neither easy nor obvious.

To see the gap between *warranted* positive (or negative) moral evaluation and justly *deserved* praise (or blame), imagine that we are in the grip of some evil demon who arbitrarily, on each individual's fortieth birthday, assigns new moral characters. Some he makes profoundly vicious. Others are profoundly virtuous—they are generous in their inclinations, their reflective deliberations affirm their virtuous inclinations, and their strong perseverance sustains those commitments under duress. Should we come to know this trickster's game but remain powerless to stop it, we should soon draw the warrants/deserves distinction quite handily. John, whom the trickster made vicious, now warrants our negative moral assessment: he is selfish, cruel, and dedicated to being so. Joan, rendered kind and generous by the same source, equally warrants our positive moral evaluations. But neither *deserves* praise or condemnation for their virtuous or vicious acts and characters. On the day following her fateful fortieth birthday we note that Joan is morally magnificent, but we should hardly conclude that she deserves praise (though she certainly warrants positive moral evaluation) for her splendid character.

Such philosophical fantasies should not be asked to bear much argumentative weight, but the burden of this story is light: it is one thing to judge someone morally good or bad, virtuous or vicious; quite another to conclude that the person deserves praise or blame, reward or punishment. Armed with the distinction between warranted and deserved moral evaluation we can deny moral responsibility and still make substantive moral evaluations.

## Justice without Just Deserts

Without moral responsibility, what becomes of justice? Some may fear that even if some moral elements can survive the demise of moral responsibility, justice would still be a casualty when just deserts are denied. If justice requires "giving to each her due," then how can there be justice if no one justly deserves reward or punishment? And if justice is lost, then fairness follows.

But the denial of moral responsibility does not imply the denial of justice and fairness; to the contrary, just deserts of reward and retribution are denied precisely *because* they are unjust and unfair. If we reject claims of miraculous self-caused willing and choosing, then close examination of individual histories reveals that we were shaped by causes beyond our control. Our virtues and vices, energy or lethargy, sagacity or impetuosity, fortitude or fluctuation: all are ultimately a matter of our good or bad fortune. Thus it is *unjust* to reward one and punish the other, as it would be unjust to reward one for a strong constitution while punishing another for frailty, and unjust to praise a tall person while condemning a short. The moral to be drawn from denial of moral responsibility is not that there is no justice or fairness, but rather that justice and fairness demand equal treatment for all, and undercut special rewards and punishments.

Some oppose the claim that justice and fairness mandate such an egalitarian system, but for the moment that is not the real issue. The point is that whatever its plausibility, the claim that we should *reject* reward and retribution because such practices are *unfair* is a coherent claim, and it is possible to maintain that an egalitarian system—premised on a *denial* of just deserts—is *fair*. Even if one holds that view to be mistaken, it is not inherently contradictory. If fairness actually required moral responsibility and just deserts, then it would be impossible to base a fairness claim on the denial of moral responsibility. But in fact it makes perfectly good sense to assert that because there is no moral responsibility, reward and retribution are *unfair* and *unjust*: true or false, the assertion is neither incoherent nor contradictory. So without moral responsibility and just deserts, we can still make meaningful claims about justice and fairness.

This is not, of course, an argument that—as a matter of objective moral fact—fairness requires the abolition of just deserts. (A more detailed examination of moral claims and moral objectivity will be the subject of the final three chapters of this book.) Neither is it claimed that an acceptable moral system must be obssessively egalitarian (possible justifications for some mild differences in benefits and detriments are discussed in chapter 8). The point here is only that moral considerations of justice and fairness can continue to be important and meaningful when moral responsibility is denied. Virtues and vices, fairness and unfairness, justice and injustice do not require a foundation of moral responsibility.

## A Glimpse of Morality without Moral Responsibility

The claim of this chapter is that denial of moral responsibility does not destroy morality. The remainder of the book pushes beyond that negative claim to a more positive view of morality. Not only can morality exist without moral responsibility; further, the vain attempt to save moral responsibility has obscured our view of the full rich range of morality and has undercut the vital foundation of moral behavior. If we must be morally responsible for our moral (and immoral) behavior, then morality itself is tightly constrained. Our feelings and affections and spontaneous nonreflective behavior are not under the control of our wills. I cannot *will* myself to feel affection where there is none, nor—as many a jilted lover will attest—can I will myself in or out of love. The moral responsibility tradition holds that I am morally responsible only for that which is within my power to will, and since (on that tradition) only behavior for which I am morally responsible can count as genuinely *moral*, the result is a severely circumscribed morality: a coldly impassive morality that overemphasizes duty and eliminates or denigrates affection and friendship and spontaneous nonreflective acts of kindness; a shallow morality cut off from its deep and sustaining biological roots.

The traditional moral responsibility model fails on two counts. First, it fails to preserve moral responsibility even in its favored domain of reflective willed duty. Second, it fails in its assumption that morality requires moral responsibility. But its baleful influence continues to shrink morality into cramped, cold, and cheerless quarters. Without moral responsibility, morality cannot only survive, but stretch and flourish—and allow itself some affections and friendships, and perhaps a lover as well. The next two chapters will examine how we animals can live morally and successfully without moral responsibility, while chapter 9 will examine the richer view of morality that results when we bring affections (and other animals) *in* and leave moral responsibility *out*.

# 7

## Moral Development
## without Moral Responsibility

The common assumption that there can be no morality without moral responsibility is supported by confusions, and the previous chapter examined the faults in that foundation. But even with the props pulled away, there remains a visceral belief that morality requires moral responsibility. The reasons offered in support of that belief fail, but belief that morality requires moral responsibility runs deeper than philosophical argument, and effective challenge of that belief requires digging it up by its roots. Those roots reach down to where morality itself developed: roots common to the mutual grooming behavior of monkeys, the rescue of group members by baboon troops, and human acts of reciprocal sharing. "You scratch my back and I'll scratch yours" (or perhaps—given the special need for cooperation in dealing with aggressors—"you watch my back and I'll watch yours"[1]): that was a literal and essential element in the development of moral behavior by our primate ancestors.[2] Examining the relation among reciprocity, just deserts, and moral development is the essential starting point for understanding the strength and depth of the false belief that morality requires moral responsibility.

The earliest instances of grooming (or defending) another were no doubt in a close-kin connection. A parent grooms a young monkey: such behavior is favored by natural selection, since those parents who give care and grooming to their young are more likely to have both their young and their genetic inclinations survive. But how was such grooming extended to nonkin?

Monkey Arnold grooms (only marginally related) monkey Ben's back. This is pleasant and advantageous for Ben, of course; but what's in it for Arnold (and Arnold's genetic legacy)? Arnold is somewhat disadvantaged (the time spent in grooming Ben cannot be used for finding food or mates) while Ben is correspondingly advantaged. If Arnold gains no advantages, then inclinations and behavior such as Arnold's will be rare: they will not endure or spread in the population.

But if Arnold more selectively grooms (or defends) only those who reciprocate, then the situation changes dramatically. If Arnold and Ben are inclined to such reciprocal cooperation, they both gain an advantage (one can more effectively groom another's back than one's own, and two heads are better than one in attacking or repelling a foe). This advantage depends on reciprocity, and on the inclination to respond reciprocally and to deny benefits to those who do not reciprocate. That is the basis for substantial development of moral behavior. Cooperation, sharing, altruism, fair play: these basic morality building blocks require inclinations toward and practice of reciprocity,[0] starting from reciprocal exchanges among kin and extending to generalized nonkin reciprocity. So there is a good explanation for the visceral sense that without reciprocity (and by extension, just deserts and retribution), there could be no morality, since reciprocity was required in order to extend morality beyond the most basic kinship regard.

Some level of simple but significant generalized (or "indirect"[4]) reciprocity is probably still required to sustain morality and moral community. In a well-functioning community, people give benefits without expecting direct returns. They buy unwanted fruit cakes from neighborhood children to support the band, even though they dislike march music; they stop to allow other vehicles into the traffic pattern, though it is unlikely that that particular driver will ever return the favor. Such generalized (indirect) reciprocity forms the cornerstone for development of morality. And the feeling of satisfaction from such simple acts of kindness marks its deep biological rootedness.

So a capacity for appreciating and selectively reciprocating benefits is basic to the development and maintenance of morality. But it is important to recognize precisely what such reciprocity is—and what it is *not*. To acknowledge the basic developmental contribution of reciprocity to morality is quite different from supposing that *moral responsibility* and *just deserts* are essential to the development of morality or its continued functioning. Exercise of (direct or indirect) reciprocity is no more moral responsibility than exchange of Christmas presents is just deserts. It is likely true that both morality and moral responsibility evolved from common reciprocity roots; but it is a mistake—a natural mistake, but no less erroneous—to equate reciprocity with the system of just deserts and retributive punishment and moral responsibility. Moral responsibility and just deserts are concerned with what is fair and just, while reciprocity is a matter of mutual benefits and social cohesiveness. To see that difference more clearly, imagine that John (who believes in moral responsibility) receives a financial favor from a mean-spirited lazy individual who holds enormous undeserved and ill-gotten wealth. John may consider it useful (both individually and socially) to *reciprocate* the favor—John may even regard such reciprocity as right and obligatory—while he vigorously denies that his benefactor *justly deserves* a reciprocal benefit. So whatever the contributions of reciprocity to morality, we cannot jump from there to the very different claim that *moral responsibility* is required for sustaining (or developing) morality.

This discussion of the development of morality has focused on reciprocal care-giving and the exchange of kindnesses, but there is a darker element that must also be considered: the exchange of hostilities. Even if it is granted that simple reciprocal exchange of favors does not make moral responsibility an essential underpinning of morality, there remains the question of whether morality requires *retributive* just deserts.

There are strong claims that retributive sentiments and practices are vital to the development of morality. J. L. Mackie offers an account of "a possible course of evolution by which retributive behavior and emotions, cooperative resentment, and the disinterested moral sentiments could have developed in turn" (Mackie 1982, 9).[5] And he specifically suggests that the retributive emotions are a more plausible path to the development of morality than is the inclination to give and return benefits:

> . . . cooperation in resentment is more likely to be useful to those who develop it than cooperation in gratitude: the repelling of injuries will often require greater concentrations of force than are needed in order to make a worthwhile return for a benefit. (Mackie 1982, 8)

Were strike-back impulses and their retributive fruits a vital building block for morality? That is a difficult empirical issue, made more imposing by the possibility that any retributive practices required for moral development might still not qualify as retributive just deserts. After all, developmentally useful strike-back responses do not automatically qualify as justly deserved retribution, just as a child's mildly painful but useful learning experience with a hot stove is not justly deserved punishment. But suppose (for the sake of argument) that Mackie's account is correct, and retribution—and cooperation in retribution—is vital to the development of morality. That would not establish that retributive moral responsibility is required for the *continued* functioning of morality. Such retributive moral responsibility might be an essential scaffolding, necessary for building moral systems; but with the systems themselves now in place, the moral responsibility scaffolding might be discarded without losing any vital support for morality.

But that leads to the real question: now that morality is developed (whether with the essential aid of retribution or not) could we pull out retributive elements without bringing down the whole structure? P. F. Strawson (1962) and Jonathan Bennett (1980a, 1980b) have addressed that question, and answered in the negative. As Bennett argues:

> The most basic way in which our willingness that a man should suffer is connected with our belief that he has offended is through their roles in adverse reactive attitudes. If I resent some attitude of yours toward me, my resentment must involve some measure of willingness that some unpleasantness should befall you. An adverse reactive attitude essentially involves some disposition to hit back or to be pleased if God or Nature does it for one. To divorce judging someone to be an offender from willingness that he should suffer, therefore, we should have to strip ourselves of all adverse reactive attitudes; and that is unthinkable or unacceptable. (1980b, 48)

So it is right that those who mistreat us experience our resentful reactions. Not because they necessarily "deserve" or will be beneficially shaped by such reactions, but rather because those who are harmed must be able to express their reactive attitudes: it is "unthinkable or unacceptable" that "we should have to strip ourselves of all adverse reactive attitudes."

Certainly the loss of "all adverse reactive attitudes" would be a substantial loss. It would impoverish our emotional lives and—for all except the purest Kantians—undercut negative moral judgments. But such a dire result does not follow from the denial of retributive just deserts. After all, we have through the centuries continued to narrow the range of suitable targets for our resentment reactive attitudes. I don't resent the river for flooding, nor the rabbit for nibbling my lettuce, nor my children for being capricious, nor the victim of a seizure for striking me while suffering an attack, nor the psychotic for his spiteful behavior, nor my friend for accidentally tripping me. Thus the sphere of proper exercise of resentful reactive attitudes has been greatly circumscribed, but without the loss of valuable reactive attitudes themselves.

Furthermore, judging that behavior does not *deserve* a resentful or strike back response (and that we should not make such a response) does not imply that there should be no reactive *feeling*. I can resent a colleague's condescending treatment—I feel the sting of such treatment, and consider it unjustified—while neither *blaming* him for his acts nor responding punitively: because, for example, I understand the desperate insecurity that drives his mean-spirited behavior. Should I be convinced that no one ever deserves to suffer—no one deserves to bear the brunt of my strikeback reactive attitude—I might continue to *feel* resentment while believing that it would be wrong to act upon it. Strong feelings (avarice and lust, for example) are not eliminated when we generally judge it better not to act on them.

Even if we did eliminate the reactive attitude of wishing to make an offender suffer, it would not follow that all adverse reactive attitudes would be lost. Whether the retributive reactive attitude is so closely yoked to other adverse reactive attitudes that they must stand or fall together is a psychobiological question, rather than a speculative philosophical one; and what evidence there is seems to indicate that the retributive attitude is not so tightly linked with the whole range of adverse reactive attitudes that they could not survive without it. As noted, we have managed substantive restrictions on our retributive reactive attitude without any corresponding reduction in all adverse reactive attitudes. Even stern retributivists now restrain their adverse reactive retributive attitudes toward those who harm by accident or seizure or insanity, and their other adverse reactive attitudes seem uncompromised by this retributive restriction. And even more to the point, there seem to be some individuals who—whether through religious influences or the teachings of behavioral psychology or the arguments of (enlightened) philosophers—do not feel a retributive reactive attitude toward wrongdoers (or who at least renounce such feelings as guides to behavior) but who continue to have strong adverse reactive attitudes against the wrongs and harms committed.

Finally, one might hold that no one is the appropriate target of resentful strike-back responses (or reward responses either, for that matter) yet still believe that such autonomous individuals are appropriate subjects for other reactive attitudes such as affection and delight, admiration and anger. A life so dominated by retributive feelings that their absence implies emotional deprivation is a sadly impoverished emotional life.

In sum, there is a good explanation of why it may *seem* obvious that moral responsibility is essential for the functioning of morality: reciprocity—from which moral responsibility notions grew and increased in stature and detail and formality—really is essential to morality and its development. But that basic reciprocity building block of morality is not moral responsibility (even though some moral responsibility notions may have been fashioned from it). Thus acknowledging that morality could not have developed (and perhaps could not be sustained) without *reciprocity* is far from supposing that *moral responsibility* is necessary for either moral development or continued moral functioning. Furthermore, retributive reciprocity *may* have been essential for the development of morality, and that also helps account for our visceral sense that morality without moral responsibility is impossible. But whatever its role in development, there is no reason to suppose that retribution is essential to *continued* functioning of morality, and there are significant reasons to suppose it is not. Thus any contribution of retributive reciprocity to development of morality counts toward explaining *away* (rather than *justifying*) the deep sense that morality requires moral responsibility.

## Real Morality without Moral Responsibility

If it is still difficult to imagine morality without moral responsibility and just deserts, perhaps that is due to a narrowly conceived notion of morality as judgment of the exact measure (rendering to each precisely her due) and following the right rules. But there is an alternative conception that makes it easier to see how morality and moral community could be sustained and supported when moral responsibility and just deserts are eliminated. Instead of the rule-following just-deserts model, consider a more nurturing (or trust-enhancing) conception of morality, of the type championed by Carol Gilligan (1982) and Annette C. Baier (1985) and Virginia Held (1990). The question, after all, is whether there could exist morality without moral responsibility: not whether some particular Kantian or utilitarian scheme could survive the demise of moral responsibility, but whether some workable morality could continue to flourish.

I am *not* willing to concede that rationalistic rule-governed moral systems require moral responsibility. It seems not unlikely that even a Kantian system (minus, of course, the harsher retributive elements) could exist without the notion of moral responsibility. (Perhaps the Kantian system might not have *developed* without moral responsibility notions, but that's another question.) But whatever the likelihood of a Kantian moral system surviving without moral responsibility, it is easy to imagine a care-based moral system—not Kantian or utilitarian, but none the worse for that—flourishing in the absence of moral responsibility.[6]

Nurture morality does not count the benefits and detriments and obligations to determine morally good acts. That is not to suggest that reciprocal kindnesses are omitted. But instead of striving for a precise quid pro quo balance, reciprocated kindnesses function to sustain cooperative behavior and strengthen appropriate trust (Baier 1985). Exact balancing and measuring is not required for the enhancing of trust and cooperation. Indeed, an exact balancing is psychologically implausible: behavior (including acts of reciprocal kindness and the trust that undergirds such acts) is more effectively and enduringly shaped by variable interval reinforcement than by exact one-to-one schedules of reward.[7]

There is no justification for moral responsibility; but there is abundant justification for simple reciprocal kindnesses, and one can consistently favor the inclination toward and practice of kind reciprocal acts while denying all just deserts ("I simply helped my friend; just deserts had nothing to do with it"). Furthermore, *generalized* (indirect) reciprocity—a key element of larger moral development—is not based on the individual desert calculations that are the core of moral responsibility. (When Edward waits to allow another motorist into traffic, he doesn't calculate the just deserts of that fellow driver; and when Beth places her life at risk in defense of her country, she does not calculate whether her compatriots justly deserve this supreme act of generalized reciprocity.)

Since reciprocity is *not* the stuff of just deserts and moral responsibility, one who rejects all moral responsibility need not oppose simple acts of reciprocal kindness. Given the denial of moral responsibility and just deserts, no one justly deserves more than another. But it does not follow that we must be obsessed with a strict and invariant egalitarian distribution, much less that we must forbid all reciprocal exchanges. As Lawrence Becker notes:

> . . . Reciprocal exchanges (of good for good) are typically a potent source of pleasure in themselves. That is, the mere transactions are a source of pleasure, independently of how highly the participants prize the things that are exchanged. (1986, 89)

So if small exceptions from a strictly egalitarian ideal are widely enjoyed and are useful in reciprocally strengthening the ties of moral community, then (even by the moral calculations of an egalitarian who steadfastly denies just deserts) such small variants may be both reasonable and morally acceptable. (This might also leave a small space for punitive responses: some mild exclusionary or even strike-back response to selfish or deleterious behavior might sometimes aid in teaching more socially beneficial behavioral patterns. If such aversive responses proved useful, that would *not* establish the usefulness of moral responsibility and just deserts: no more than the usefulness of a slight burn for a child learning to avoid hot radiators proves that the child justly deserves to be burned.) Thus small variance of benefits (and mildly punitive-aversive responses) can be admitted without assuming or allowing moral responsibility. There may be a question of whether such small variations from egalitarian distribution are morally justified by the reciprocal strengthening of moral community; but the point is that ruling out just deserts and moral responsibility will not automatically rule out such reciprocal exchanges. A nurture ethics may celebrate reciprocal, trust-enhancing acts of kindness without embracing dutiful just deserts.

Clearly, then, a trust or nurture ethics (while it might employ some reciprocity) does not require the strict and elaborate machinery of moral responsibility. But it may be objected that while a nurture ethics has its charms, it is not empirically likely that such a moral system could have developed in social reality. Wouldn't individuals have learned (or evolved) to give minimally, thus undermining nurturing reciprocity and replacing it with narrow reciprocity (or strict just deserts)?

The objection that animals (including human animals) would undermine simple nurture-enhancing reciprocity by "minimal giving" fails for at least three reasons. First, a major part of the evolution of moral behavior most likely involved subtle but powerful selection pressures in favor of the capacity to detect and avoid shirkers and manipulators and minimizers (Trivers 1971). Second—a result closely tied to the first reason—such calculation of minimums would probably be a losing strategy. As Richard Alexander notes, where social and reciprocal interactions are complex and extended the calculator of minimal reciprocity is likely to miscalculate. In any case, "astute observers would avoid him in future interactions in favor of others more likely to be more beneficent or less careful about their own or immediate self-interests, and he could lose mightily on that account." Thus "his tendency to be a conscious, deliberate, cynical, cost-benefit tester in each circumstance would cause him to lose" (1987, 119). The contrast with the situation of the less calculating and more generous (trust-enhancing) individual is dramatic:

> If he occasionally erred in the specific situation on the side of beneficence this would label him as a good interactant to seek out, and one to whom help could be given with little fear of being short-changed. (Alexander 1987, 119)

Finally, the suggestion that generous reciprocity would be undercut by stingy minimal reciprocity betrays a naive view of the evolution of behavior. The evolution of such *minimal* reciprocity would require that reciprocity be controlled by a single genetic factor, with the minimum-reciprocity-allele enjoying an evolutionary advantage over (and eventually eliminating) the generous-nurturing-reciprocity tendency. But such complex behaviors as nurturing and reciprocity are not under the control of a single on-off allele. To the contrary, their development is part of a larger pattern involving care for young, social cooperation, desire for and pleasure in society, affection for family and community members, and recognition of and sympathetic participation in the sufferings and pleasures of others. Thus one cannot pull out the single reciprocity thread and shorten it to minimal length: it is woven into a larger and more complex fabric.

Whatever the survivability of nurture morality, there may still be a sense that *real* morality—in our harsh gritty world—must be tough Kantian rule-governed morality or strict utilitarian calculations. But in fact the nurturing model is a more accurate reflection of the actual development of morality: not from a social contract, in which rational creatures sat together to draw up rules that transformed them from brutish and callous to cooperative and caring; but instead through the extension of nurturing behavior that originally developed out of family and kin and group relations.[8] Nurture morality emphasizes (Baier 1985) the development of conditions under which appropriate (generously reciprocated) care and trust (rather than rules and duties) are generated and fostered. Thus the nurturing model matches the empirical reality of our development as moral animals, and avoids the idealizations of exaggerated rational rule-following and calculations. Rationalistic models—whether Kantian-principled or consequentialist-calculating[9]—set humans and the human creation of morality apart from the evolution and behavior of other animals, while the nurture model stays close to the caring and nurturing behavior that humans share with many other species. If one regards humans as radically or miraculously separate, then the rule-governed models will be more appealing. Post-Darwinians who believe humans and human behavior evolved with other animals in the natural world might well find the nurturing model more plausible.

For those who affirm close connections rather than vast divides between humans and other animals (and between human *moral* behavior and the behavior of other animals), there is a final reason for maintaining that morality does not require moral responsibility. As Michael Ruse notes:

> Darwinism insists that features evolve gradually, and something as important as morality should have been present in our (very recent) shared ancestors. Furthermore, if morality is as important biologically to humans as is being claimed, it would be odd indeed had all traces now been eliminated from the social interactions of other high-level primates. (Ruse 1986, 227)

And as Ruse notes, we now have evidence of such moral behavior in other animals:

> Apes interact in remarkably human-like fashions, including fashions which, were we to believe them true of humans (rather than apes), we would unhesitatingly label "moral." (Ruse 1986, 228)

But it is one thing to suggest that apes may behave morally or immorally; it is quite another to suppose that they are morally responsible (deserve punishment or reward) for their moral or immoral behavior. Of course some will deny that other animals behave morally, and there may be those who ascribe morality to nonhuman animals and also hold them morally responsible. Both views seem implausible to me, but they need not be critiqued here. The immediate point is just that the question of whether other animals act *morally* is different and distinct from the question of whether they are *morally responsible*. Maintaining that other animals have at least a rudimentary morality does not imply that they are morally responsible, and that is sufficient to show that morality does not require moral responsibility.

### The Tasks of Morality

Belief that denial of moral responsibility destroys morality is based on confusions. Without moral responsibility and just deserts, autonomous individuals can act morally and immorally, be virtuous and vicious, and have a rich moral language. The burden of proof now rests on those who would claim that loss of moral responsibility entails loss of morality. And that burden is made heavier by examples of moral actors (vicious Elaine, virtuous Carol, and perhaps also Washoe and Mama) whose moral responsibility has been called into question.

Some may still suppose that morality-without-moral-responsibility could only exist in hothouse philosophical theory: it could not survive in real-world practice, since there would be no way to sustain virtuous behavior or stop vicious, no means of expressing our deepest moral principles and commitments and evaluations, no resources to manifest our outrage at vicious violations of our morality nor our joy at splendid manifestations of virtue.[10] In a society without just deserts (so the objection goes), morality could not flourish nor even function.

But in fact there are substantive real-life tasks for morality when it gets out of the business of praising and condemning and rewarding and punishing. There remain moral decisions to be made, examined, and critiqued, as well as a need for moral evaluations of characters: characters that may *warrant* positive or negative moral assessments without justly deserving either reward or blame. Furthermore, while punishing malefactors and rewarding moral excellence is one way of asserting and celebrating our moral commitments, it is a comparatively weak and ineffectual one. Punishing and blaming may be more detrimental than beneficial in reforming behavior, and typically such use of "just deserts" leaves the causal factors intact to continue shaping vicious character. A more convincing and effective demonstration of moral disgust involves seeking out and changing those causal conditions. The absence of just deserts prompts deeper examination of the causal factors that shape and sustain virtuous and vicious character and behavior, and deeper examination of causes reveals better strategies to strengthen virtue and enfeeble vice.[11] And finally, without moral responsibility, there remain the basic elements of morality that traditional moral philosophy has typically ignored or disparaged: the nurturing and trust-building that thrives on simple reciprocities but is stifled by strict demands of eye-for-an-eye "justice."

We do not need moral responsibility—with its cargo of retributive punishment, differential rewards, and inegalitarian distributive justice—for securing what most will find genuinely valuable: the capacity to be a moral agent, to make moral choices and moral evaluations and moral commitments, to take (take-charge) responsibility for our own moral characters and exercise autonomous control over our own choices and values, to effectively combat vice, to nurture and strengthen affection, and to shape virtuous behavior in ourselves and others. Without just deserts, there remains much for morality to do, and it is likely to be done better without the unwieldy weight of moral responsibility: a weight that threatens to drag morality back into mysteries, and at best obscures the deeper causal factors that we must examine to effectively enhance moral character and virtuous behavior and appropriate trust. We can cherish and strengthen both morality and the simple warm reciprocities that sustain moral community while we dance on the grave of moral responsibility.

# 8

---

## Bitter Fruits, Just Deserts, and Natural Consequences

The development of morality probably involved reciprocity. Such reciprocity is not just deserts, but it does involve experiencing consequences (when kind or unkind deeds are reciprocated). Such simple reciprocity cannot establish just deserts and moral responsibility; but many think otherwise, and they attempt to squeeze just deserts through the reciprocity opening. If reciprocity is developmentally useful, does that justify experiencing the consequences of one's behavior and ultimately the *just deserts* for one's acts?

Should we experience the results of our choices, enjoy the fruits of our labors, and suffer the consequences of our misdeeds? The affirmative answer is widely accepted, both within and without philosophical reflection. But closer scrutiny is needed, for two reasons. First, if Heloise is severely injured while saving a child from the path of a train, few would claim that she *should* suffer the injurious consequences of her heroic act. Thus the principle that people should experience the effects of their behavior requires some obvious (and less than obvious) modifications. Second, there are problems with what is assumed to follow from the principle: namely, just deserts and moral responsibility.

### Free Choice and Choice-Consequences

The value of experiencing the "choice-consequences" of one's choices and behavior is more often assumed than argued. But of the arguments offered, one of the most promising is: the value of experiencing choice-consequences is an inseparable element of the value of free choice itself.

A choice without effects is a choice in only a Pickwickian sense. Consider a child who is told that she may freely choose whether to eat her candy but has it taken away because she "made the wrong choice." The unfortunate child has been deprived of both candy and choice, since a choice stripped of all consequences is at best a pale imitation of the real thing. George Sher makes the point cogently:

> Because we deliberate with an eye to consequences, our free choices must encompass not just our immediate doings, but also the later lines of development to which we expect them to lead. Thus, at least one connection between free acts and their consequences is internal to the notion of free agency itself.
>
> And, given this connection, we can indeed see why any value that attaches to an autonomous act might carry over to that act's consequences. . . . Since choices encompass both acts and consequences, any value that attaches to the implementation of choice must belong equally to both. (Sher 1987, 39 40)

Assume it generally desirable—as part of the desirability of free choice—that people receive the foreseeable fruits of their choices and behavior. That will not take us very far. Valuing free choices and their foreseeable consequences is one thing, while valuing unforeseen consequences is quite another. I value choosing an egg salad sandwich for lunch; and obviously part of that value is actually eating the sandwich I choose. But choosing egg salad does not confer value on the unforeseen consequence of developing food poisoning nor on the unanticipated long-term result of high cholesterol.

There is, however, a second source for the value of choice-consequences, and it may support even unforeseen consequences. Choice-consequences are a means of shaping behavior, and it is generally advantageous that behavior be shaped in accordance with its natural consequences. The world will be more congenial for those whose behavior has been shaped by that world's natural contingencies, and the benefits extend to unforeseen consequences. When I pull my head up to watch the flight of my golf ball, I do not foresee that the result will be a pathetic shot that dribbles five yards off the tee, but that unpleasant consequence may nonetheless be an effective reminder to keep my head down.

We want to be shaped by our real environment. Artificial or deceptive manipulations cause well-grounded concern. Overprotective parents (who insulate their children from the unpleasant consequences of foolish behavior) do a disservice to their children, whose unrealistic sugarplum childhood shapes behavioral patterns ill-suited for the harsher environmental reality. The teacher who praises shoddy performance reinforces behavior that will ultimately prove deleterious. And one of the deep fears of any "virtual reality" pleasure machine (in which I experience unmixed pleasure and excitement, with little effort and less frustration) is that it shapes behavior for an unreal world: behavior that will be treated severely by the real environment in which we ultimately must live our lives and measure our successes.

It is unfortunate when indulgent parents inadvertently shape counterproductive behavior, but greater danger lurks in artificially contrived environments that purposefully employ short-term reinforcement patterns to shape people to their long-term detriment. Under a piecework system, for example, the factory worker initially completes a small number of units to earn a bonus; gradually (as the worker's speed increases) the number of units required to receive the reward is increased. This "stretched-interval" pattern of reinforcement subtly shapes workers who exert great effort for small reward. The long-term results are ruinous to the exhausted workers who are ultimately cast aside (Skinner 1971, 34–35). The process is facilitated by a double dose of contrived contingencies: the stretched interval reinforcement pattern is artificially contrived, and the rewards are also artificial (there is nothing inherently reinforcing about the tokens given for completing the prescribed production units). Such a situation divorces workers from the natural rewards of their work, and their behavior is controlled by a manipulated environment that makes them particularly vulnerable to exploitation.

Thus there are good and sufficient reasons to want our behavior shaped for success in the real world in which we live, rather than in a hothouse setting that overindulges us or a contrived setting that may manipulate us to our ultimate detriment. But there are problems attached to the benefits of natural consequences. It is true that natural consequences often shape desirable adaptive behavior. Just as natural consequences may yield a species successfully adapted to its environment, so natural short-term (learning) contingencies may shape an individual that responds to its environment in ways that are optimally rewarded. But the evolutionary process wastes a multitude of misfits in the process, and often sends species down evolutionary dead ends; likewise, natural short-term consequences may produce a multitude of misshapen individuals for every successful adaptation and may also lead to long-term disaster.

We want to be shaped for success in the real world, but that important truth is tangled with a subtle mistake: the mistaken assumption that the natural arrangement of natural consequences is the best way of shaping success in the natural world. It is a mistake to turn the shaping of good and effective behavior over to the laissez-faire guidance of natural consequences, for a simple but too easily overlooked reason: remote long-term behavioral effects may be so remote that they fail to shape successful behavioral adaptations (just as the long-term detriments of laboring at stretched-interval piecework are masked by immediate short-term rewards). The immediate natural consequences of inhaling cigarette smoke are positively reinforcing. The taste is pleasant and the nicotine refreshing, and those effects shape dedicated smokers. The long-term effects are decidedly less appealing. The solution is not in letting the "natural" consequences run their course. Requiring the long-term smoker to suffer untreated cancer is both cruel and ineffectual, since any shaping of smoking cessation occurs much too late.

The benefits of natural arrangements of natural consequences are problematic at best, and the problems are exacerbated when we include natural *social* consequences. Social consequences form a substantive part of our natural environment. After all, "natural consequences" does not mean consequences "untouched by human hand"; if it did, the category of natural consequences would be very thinly populated, since most of the consequences we experience have been developed or at least filtered through human society. But our natural social environment is not naturally suited for shaping successful long-term behavior. The problems with the "natural" arrangement of social consequences is nowhere more evident than in the common social practices of reward and punishment, praise and blame. It may be natural to rebuke and praise, but it is another matter to suppose that that socially conditioned natural tendency is therefore advantageous and desirable.

It is hardly surprising that a system that makes liberal use of reward and punishment should have become dominant. It is counterproductive at worst, profligate with human resources at best, and basically unjust in any case; but it has not had much competition, and it generates sufficient short-term success to keep it in force. When pleasing behavior is rewarded, it is more likely to occur, and the rebuking or punishing of unwanted behavior may immediately reduce that behavior. Thus while punitive responses may cause long-term problems, they are likely to yield short-term benefits for the punisher (the immediate source of unpleasantness is often eliminated); and immediate, short-term success is enough to sustain punitive behavioral patterns. But while it may be easily understood why such a system of reward and punishment might endure (and why a morality of "just deserts" might develop around it), the inefficiency of the punishment-reward system is also obvious.

To see the flaws in our traditional "natural" system of reward and punishment in accordance with "deserts," consider two marathoners of very different abilities. The gifted runner's desultory performance outdistances the field and wins reward; but the reward functions to reinforce slipshod effort, and discourages the athlete from achieving her best. Her hard-training competitor is woefully limited in ability and consistently finishes among the last stragglers, and the long-term absence of positive reinforcement eventually extinguishes this plodder's capacity to exert heroic efforts. Obviously there are cases in which people are rewarded and rebuked (under the system of "just deserts") in a manner that shapes heroic efforts and record-breaking runs. And in the absence of anything better, those benefits will entrench the system. But such successes are purchased at the price of enormous waste.

In sum, there is an important truth beneath the idea that it is beneficial for people to experience and be shaped by the natural choice-consequences of their behavior. We want to be shaped for success in our real environment, and thus shaped in accordance with the real forces and actual consequences of that environment. But that is not best achieved by "letting nature take its consequential course." First, the supposed "hands-off" approach still involves contrived social consequences that are applied ineffectively; and second, such a laissez-faire approach fails to address the problem of bringing behavior under the effective control of long-term consequences.

## Natural Consequences and Just Deserts

There are benefits to experiencing the consequences of one's choices, but choice-consequences are neither an unmixed good nor an easy path to virtue. Some may object, however, that such considerations are irrelevant: you simply *deserve* the choice-consequences of your acts; the foundation for choice-consequences is not benefit or convenience but *justice*.

Attempts to justify choice-consequences as beneficial in shaping effective behavior are at best a limited success; attempts to justify choice-consequences as fair and just are a total failure. It is sometimes useful that people experience the effects of their choices, but it does not follow that they *deserve* the results of their choices. I attend a party in the company of Bertie Wooster (the endearingly scatterbrained hero of many P. G. Wodehouse novels); both of us drink to excess, in full and bitter knowledge of the painful consequences. But Bertie enjoys the services of the inimitable Jeeves, who Bertie foresees will concoct a wonderful potion to mitigate the baleful results of overindulgence. I, having no such potion available, shall suffer more severely (as I also foresee). But having overindulged from the same motives and to the same degree, surely I do not *deserve* to suffer more.

Again, suppose that we are hiking on a summer day. With full knowledge that the trek is long, the day is hot, and the water is limited, you carefully conserve your water while I quickly drain my canteen. During the remainder of the hike, you are refreshed by cool draughts while I suffer increasing thirst (being loathe to deny me the full value of my free choice, you decline to share your water with me). We both made choices, and with full knowledge of the consequences. Do I now deserve to endure thirst, while you deserve the benefits of conserving your water?

This is not a dispute over the usefulness of my suffering thirst. Perhaps plodding through the trip with no water will "teach me a lesson," and I shall learn better self-control; if so, it may be useful for me to suffer the consequences of my short-sighted choices and intemperate behavior. Possibly the experience of thirst will have the opposite effect: I become even less self-controlled, more obsessively concerned with immediate gratification, and take less heed for the morrow. But that difference in what is learned makes no difference in my just *deserts.* If I *deserve* to be thirsty, that doesn't change whether the experience teaches me something or not.[1]

If questions concerning the learning benefits of choice-consequences are set aside, the severe problems with linking just deserts and choice-consequences soon become clear. Examining the contrast between my intemperance and your careful rationing, the question must soon arise: *why* do you have such powers of self-control, and why do I take the ultimately more painful path of immediate self-gratification? The causes of our different choices are not difficult to trace. You learned self-control as your early choices of delayed gratification were rewarded (perhaps by a loving parent, who not only provided the immediate reinforcement of lavish praise when you saved your cookies until after dinner, but also added an ice cream bonus with your cookie dessert); I learned intemperance when the cookies I saved were stolen by my greedy sibling. If that is oversimplified, the point is nonetheless a simple one. Whether one has or has not learned the valuable lessons of self-control is a matter of one's fortunate or unfortunate learning history, and that history is not of one's own making: it is a matter of good or bad fortune, of "grace, not works, lest any man should boast." And the same is true not only of instances requiring self-control, but also for related questions concerning powers of careful deliberation and strength of will. If one person deliberates carefully (examining the long-term and short-term consequences, considering all the possibilities, weighing the options) while another chooses rashly, the same questions of learning history arise, and analogous answers remain the most plausible: answers that undermine claims of moral responsibility and just deserts.

Yet another problem confronts those who would base just deserts on the natural benefits and detriments that result from deliberate behavior. In many cases, the consequences may be so rewarding or (more likely, given the hardness of the world and its gods) so punitive that even the stern champion of just deserts must doubt that the deliberate actor deserves such consequences. Sher wrestles honestly with that problem and offers the following excellent example. A man drives his truck out onto the ice after some unseasonably warm weather; the ice cracks, and the truck goes into the lake. This foolish behavior elicits a letter to the editor: after the recent warm weather "anyone who is crazy enough to drive their vehicle out on the ice deserves to have the vehicle go through the ice." Sher claims that his "expected-consequences account" of desert will accommodate the intuitions of this letter writer, as well as other important beliefs about deserts:

> Just as the man who leaves his umbrella home when it rains deserves to get wet, so too does the man who brings his umbrella deserve to reach his destination dry. More important, we believe that persons who resourcefully seize opportunities deserve the resulting benefits, that persons who carefully make and execute plans deserve success, and that persons who forego immediate benefits in expectation of longer-range gains deserve those gains. In all such cases, the expected-consequence account explains not only why the deserving party should have something, but also why he should have what we intuitively feel he deserves. (Sher 1987, 41–2)

But Sher recognizes that such examples also pose problems for his expected-consequences account of just deserts:

> We may agree that the ice fisherman who has not first tested the ice deserves to lose his truck, but few would say that he deserves to lose his life. Even if both outcomes are equally predictable, the latter desert-claim seems unduly harsh. Similarly, we would balk at the claim that a daredevil who tries to leap a twenty-foot chasm deserves to be paralyzed, or that a heavy smoker deserves to get lung cancer. In part, our hesitation may reflect doubt that these outcomes are predictable with sufficient certainty, but it also has another explanation: that any value which these outcomes inherit is overmatched by their disvalue. To say that personal autonomy is a great good is not to deny that suffering and death are great evils. Thus, when a free act's consequences include such misfortunes, there comes a point at which the value they inherit from the agent's exercise of freedom is outweighed by their intrinsic disvalue. Hence, the feeling that such consequences are not deserved is only to be expected. Far from damaging the expected-consequence account, this intuition is a harmless manifestation of the plurality of value. (Sher 1987, 45–46)

But if expected consequences confer just deserts, it would be more plausible to say that the individual deserves to drown or be paralyzed or develop lung cancer, notwithstanding other reasons for hoping that the individual does not get what he or she deserves. It is difficult—for me, at least—to suppose that anyone justly deserves to die for failing to check the thickness of ice, or to imagine that anyone would count such a death as justly deserved. On the other hand, if the unfortunate ice fisherman does *not* deserve such harsh results, that is not a "harmless manifestation of the plurality of value" but instead a strong counterexample to Sher's expected-consequences account of just deserts.

### Investment Returns and Just Deserts

The sense that one *must* justly deserve the consequences of one's choices is stubborn, and is held in place by another deep assumption: it is right and just that people receive choice-conse-quences as *fair returns* on their investments. The idea has deep roots: "Whatsoever a man soweth, that also shall he reap." When we make choices and act on those choices, we make investments of our time and effort and resources. Sher insists that the diligent ought to reap the benefits of their choices and efforts because:

> . . . their sustained efforts are substantial investments of themselves—the ultimate sources of value—in the outcomes they seek. (1987, 62)

That being the case, we deserve reward because we are entitled to a just return on our investment. (Or—As Hegel asserted—the malefactor has a *right* to claim just punishment.)

As direct and appealing as this fair-investment-return argument appears at first glance, its flaws soon become evident. The justice of receiving choice-consequences cannot be based on investment returns. May is given a million dollars to invest, and June receives a thousand. Both make their respective investments and receive proportionate returns. Does May then deserve a thousandfold more than June? Obviously not, unless both *deserve* their starting capital.

Assuming that capital acquired in standard legitimate ways (through inheritance or ingenuity, hard work or good luck) is *justly* one's own, then questions about the fairness of the ini-tial capital acquisition can be left aside. But the issue here is more basic, and no foundation of just capital accumulation can be assumed. Examining how we acquire "capital" for investment of *ourselves* swiftly undermines claims that differences in character capital investment can justify different consequential returns. May has more capital available for investment than does June: she invests greater diligence, deeper thought, broader knowledge, and shrewder judgment than does June, and it is not surprising that the returns on her richer investment are more favorable. But unless one can swallow the mysteries of *ab initio* self-made selves and uncaused causes, then May's admirable investment portfolio is the product of her genetic endowment nurtured by a supportive and stimulating early environment, and that hardly seems grounds for May to claim that she now justly deserves more than June (whose investment resources are considerably smaller).

Not all of May's investment capital was inherited, of course; she developed some of her good qualities through hard work. And some of June's inherited wealth—her "god-given talents"—may have been squandered through sloth or drink. But when we look more carefully at May's diligence and June's lethargy, it is clear that such characteristics cannot support just deserts returns on personal investments. As already noted, diligence (and lethargy) are also products of our good (or bad) fortune in the way our characters and capacities were shaped. Diligence is an important characteristic, and certainly much can be accomplished by means of this admirable quality. But what is accomplished—through personal investments of talents and diligence—is not entitled to "just deserts" returns.

Someone might claim that full receipt of choice-consequences will encourage wise and vigorous investments, but that argument has already been tried and found wanting. It is not an efficient means of shaping optimal behavior (the affluent may be shaped to lethargic and slipshod investment of their rich resources, while the less-talented lose all inclination to invest); and even if it were effective, that would not justify claims of just deserts and moral responsibility.

## Consequences and Accountability

It is difficult to shake the persistent attachment to choice-consequences: not just the sense of *wanting* to experience my own choice-consequences, but a stronger sense that I *should.* Some of this stubborn valuing is tied to the value of responsibility and accountability.

Being responsible for our acts and choices is the price as well as the ticket to the community of self-governing, responsibility-accepting, fully functioning individuals. And part of the value of taking responsibility for our choices and acts is valuing the *consequences* of the choices that we claim as our own. But while the value of personal responsibility and accountability provides some justification for choice-consequences, it cannot provide the wholesale justification that is often supposed; and in particular, it cannot justify the full panoply of choice-consequences demanded by just deserts.

Our legitimate interest in responsibility and accountability cannot support the choice-consequences associated with just deserts. Understanding why requires one last look at the treacherous ambiguity in "responsibility": between take-charge responsibility and moral (just-deserts) responsibility. When Professor Pangloss suffers severe problems (profound and debilitating depression, for example), he may still have responsibility for grade reports; but while Professor Pangloss is responsible (*take-charge* responsible) for submitting grades, he is not responsible (*morally* responsible, deserving of blame or credit) for failing to do so.

On a larger scale, Candide has responsibility for himself: he makes his own decisions, takes responsibility for his life and his plans, and does not want—would bitterly resent—interference with his life and his choices. "I make my own decisions, and I take responsibility for them": so Candide asserts if anyone attempts to run his life. But just as in the case of Professor Pangloss, Candide may have take-charge responsibility for his life while obviously not having *moral* responsibility (not *deserving* blame for his faults nor bad consequences for his failures). Candide has his problems, but he is at least minimally competent, and he legitimately demands and values take-charge responsibility for his own life. He would be frustrated by paternalistic intervention, and since we value individual autonomy and decision-making (and obviously the value of such autonomous decision making does not depend on perfect rationality in the decision maker), it is better to have Candide make his own decisions whenever possible. (We typically value such choice making as a good-in-itself, and choice-making *practice* improves one's autonomy skills.) But given Candide's traumatic youthful experiences, Candide should surely not be blamed for making bad choices. They are his choices, and it is good that he have the opportunity to make them; and since choice-conse-quences often are part of the value of choices, it is often desir-able for Candide to experience those consequences; but he does not *deserve* the bad results from his bad choices.

Take-charge responsibility for one's choices and their con-sequences is valuable and remains valuable in the absence of moral responsibility. To go further, take-charge responsibility is valuable even for acts and consequences that are *not* the result of one's deliberative choices. Such take-charge responsibility is a vital element in having a sense of one's self as an actor who makes things happen, instead of a passive victim. In the words of Bernard Williams, responsibility is an essential element of being a "mature agent":

> The mature agent . . . will recognize his relation to his acts in their undeliberated, and also in their unforeseen and unin-tended aspects. He recognizes that his identity as an agent is constituted by more than his deliberative self. . . . The agent lives with the truth that his character, what he is, is neither a deliberative construct of his, nor fully expressed in his delib-erations. . . . He will be able to acknowledge more generally that he can be as responsible for some things that he did not intend as much as he is for things that he did intend. . . . For him, to be responsible is not simply to be properly held responsible by others, by the institutions of control and cohe-sion, but to hold himself responsible. . . . No conception of public responsibility can match exactly an ideal of maturity because, among other reasons, to hold oneself responsible only when the public could rightfully hold one responsible is not a sign of maturity. (Williams 1985/1995, 32)

Thus it is often healthy and "mature" to acknowledge that an act is one's own and the consequences are of one's own doing, even when the action is unintended and undeliberated and the results unforeseen. Those who fail to acknowledge and claim their undeliberated acts suffer a limited and enfeebled range of acknowledged action, and they often approach the world as passive victims rather than active and effective participants. Embracing the full rich range of choices and actions—including those that are not deliberative and some that are not even intended—enriches take-charge responsibility for self and enlarges interaction with the world and its options. But healthy and mature as such responsibility acknowledgment may be, it is a valuable form of take-charge responsibility: *not* a means of enlarging moral responsibility. It is psychologically healthy, morally mature, and behaviorally effective for Candide to acknowledge his unintended acts as his own and to claim authority over and responsibility (take-charge responsibility) for them; but that take-charge responsibility cannot justify anyone else in either praising or blaming Candide for such acts, nor can it justify Candide in claiming that he deserves reward (or deserves punishment) for such unintended acts. One can *take* take-charge responsibility for both intended and unintended acts; one can take *moral* responsibility for neither.

One may have take-charge responsibility, then, for making decisions about how best to live one's life ("I take responsibility for my own life, I make my own decisions, and should you want an *account* of my choices, ask *me*"); but not deserve blame or credit (and not *deserve* the choice-consequences) for one's decisions and their effects. And this is a difference that makes a difference. For example, many now call for patients to take more responsibility (take-charge responsibility) for their own health care: individuals should keep their own medical histories, watch their own diets and medications, and make their own decisions concerning medical treatment. Such increased (take-charge) responsibility may indeed be good. People will learn to take better care of themselves, and having greater control of one's own medical care may lessen the depressing sense of helplessness that often accompanies and hinders treatment. But it does not justify the *moral* responsibility that is frequently assumed to follow. "I take (take-charge) responsibility for my own health decisions; thus I am responsible (morally responsible, justly deserving of the results) for the effects of my smoking and high-fat diet and should not expect expensive bypass surgery nor access to scarce transplant organs, but should instead suffer the deserved effects of my poor choices." When the distinction between take-charge responsibility and just-deserts responsibility is marked, it is obvious that that is a non sequitur.

Along similar lines, if we acknowledge the legitimate take-charge responsibility of many nonhuman animals for their own lives, that will be strong grounds for avoiding interference in their lives and choices. But it will not follow that nonhuman animals deserve the suffering they may endure as a result of unfortunate choices, and if we can alleviate such suffering without undue damage to their autonomous exercise of take-charge responsibility, then we should provide such relief—for humans as well as members of other species.

Accountability and take-charge responsibility—even take-charge responsibility for self—will not justify claims of just deserts: will not establish that one *deserves* to suffer or enjoy the consequences of one's choices. Nonetheless, respect for individual take-charge responsibility provides strong support for choice-consequences. Intervention to cancel out the consequences of my take-charge responsible choices may be rightly resented. As noted at the beginning of the chapter, the consequences of our choices are sometimes an indivisible element of the choices themselves and thus share the value of our choice making. And for us take-charge responsible sorts, the value of choice making is a substantive value indeed. (Not some mysterious, transcendent sort of choice making: simple choice making in accordance with my own conditioned ordinary motives has great and sufficient charms.) So even though no one *deserves* the choice-consequences of her acts and choices, it is valuable   and valuable in a way that goes beyond merely useful—that we (and other take-charge responsible animals) generally experience the choice-consequences of our acts.

But this is not a justification of just deserts. Choice-consequences are differential consequences, while in just deserts everyone is equal. So rather than choice-consequences justifying just deserts, the desirability of choice-consequences may sometimes override the value of *just* (that is, *equal*) deserts. And if we bear that in mind, we shall no longer be tempted to extravagant demands that everyone must receive the full measure of choice-consequences of their acts. Such choice-consequences are often desirable and valuable, but they are not morally mandatory. Thus when differences among choice-consequences leave some severely—and *unjustly*—disadvantaged, it is legitimate to correct such imbalances. And when the choice-consequences are such as to override any desirability or value derived from the choice itself, there will be no temptation to suppose that just deserts requires draining the consequences to the bitter dregs.

## Paternalism

Take-charge responsibility will not establish that one *deserves* to suffer or enjoy the consequences of one's choices, but take-charge responsibility is an important element in understanding the value of choice-consequences as well as the dangers of paternalism. Paternalism is a legitimate concern. If I have decided to skip my annual physical, then—as a minimally competent take-charge responsible individual—that foolish choice is my own. If you coerce me into taking a physical, then whatever the benefit of that paternalistic intervention, it will have the detrimental effect of denying my autonomy and my free choice and my (take-charge) responsibility for myself. I resent your paternalistic treatment (though I do not *blame* you for it) and rightly feel that you have deprived me of something important: the opportunity to make my own choice, even a foolish one. If this pattern is played out on a large scale, the result is a denial of my take-charge responsibility for my self, and that will be a serious loss indeed. But there are two things to note regarding such paternalism.

First, the problems of paternalism do not involve just deserts and moral responsibility. Paternalism threatens autonomy and take-charge responsibility for self, and moral responsibility has nothing to do with it. Alice is competent and deliberative. She chooses to forgo heart transplant surgery, believing that she has lived a full span and that limited medical resources should be used for others. We might well honor her decision though we disagree with it. We think she is unwisely depriving herself of several years of productive and pleasurable life, but the decision is her own and respect for her autonomy and her take-charge responsibility for self supersede the advantages of paternalistic intervention. But whether she *deserves* the effects of her autonomous choice is another matter altogether. If one calculates in terms of just deserts, one might claim that this noble and courageous woman deserves a longer life and deserves it more than someone who chooses to clutch at life without regard to the just distribution of limited lifesaving resources. Obviously, then, autonomy and just deserts are not so tightly linked as the tradition has assumed.

Second, intervention to prevent someone experiencing choice-consequences is not always a paternalistic denial of autonomy. In some circumstances it may enhance rather than undermine autonomy. If I choose to go mountain climbing and you paternalistically deny me that opportunity, then you have restricted my autonomy and usurped at least part of my take-charge responsibility for myself. But suppose that no one interferes with my foolish mountain-climbing decision, and then the predicted blizzard strikes and leaves me snowbound and isolated. I now call back to the lodge for help: I am asking for aid in escaping the natural consequences (miserable hours of cold, perhaps frostbite, possibly death) of my foolish choice to go mountain climbing. If you answer my call and rescue me from my predicament, then your intervention would hardly be paternalistic. (Of course it would be a different story if I steadfastly insisted that I wanted no rescuers.) To the contrary, you enhance my autonomy by enlarging my options and opportunities: you add an opportunity (for escape) that I desire, and the opportunity is added at my specific request. Indeed, even if I foresaw the consequences of my mountaineering expedition—I anticipated being caught in a blizzard and thought it would be a noble way to die—and now change my mind, call for help, and a rescue squad intervenes to save me from those foreseen consequences, my autonomy is still enhanced (rather than denied by paternalistic interference).

There is nothing magical about natural consequences, particularly about the "natural" consequences of reward and retribution. The system of moral responsibility and "getting what you deserve" impedes attempts to shape behavior for long-term success. Natural consequences have their uses, but they may also shape superstition and lethargy, cruelty and hopelessness. It can be both satisfying and beneficial to experience the natural effects of our choices and acts, and such experience can enhance individual autonomous take-charge-responsible choice within an environment that shapes effective long-term behavior. But such values do not require the full measure of choice-consequences as "just deserts." Choice-consequences are often valuable, but just deserts are neither just nor deserved nor beneficial.

# 9

---

## Morality without Reason

A world without moral responsibility is a congenial habitat for autonomous moral animals, but a basic question remains: What sort of morality will they practice? That is, what moral system fits the Darwinist world view?

Darwinism has important implications for morality, but not the implications popularly associated with Darwinism. At one extreme, we cannot simply read off moral truths from Darwinism: there is no "Darwinist ethics" (social Darwinist or otherwise) that follows from Darwinism. But while Darwinism does not support a special moral system—and certainly not a brutal might-makes-right war of all-against-all—neither does it reduce morality to idle fantasy. Darwinism does not establish any moral truths, but it enriches and expands our moral perspective.

What Darwinism contributes to our understanding of morality is a much-debated question, and one that will be closely considered in the final chapters. But whether one takes the pro or con view on the evolutionary contribution to understanding morality, there is typically an underlying assumption shared by both sides: whatever is or is not learned about morality from evolutionary biology, the morality itself is the exclusive domain of the human species. Other animals may or may not have rights to human consideration, but only humans are moral, and only humans behave morally or immorally. Dogs may be affectionate, but their affection is not exercise of virtue. Chimps may carry out heroic rescues of their young, but they cannot have the virtue of heroism—at best, they have the semblance of that virtue. An orangutan may be vicious, but cannot have a vice. Or so the tradition holds. But such a sharp division between humans and the rest of the natural world prompts Darwinian suspicions. Is it plausible to separate human moral behavior so absolutely from the behavior of all other animals? Or is this another of the variety of principles humans have proposed to secure our unique status: we are God's special creation, and the natural world is made for our use; we have souls, the animals are merely machines; of all the animals, only humans are blessed with autonomy; we have reason, others only instinct; and we alone are moral.

The implausibility of this radical "humans are moral/animals are nonmoral" distinction has been noted by Michael Ruse:

> Darwinism insists that features evolve gradually, and something as important as morality should have been present in our (very recent) shared ancestors. Furthermore, if morality is as important biologically to humans as is being claimed, it would be odd indeed had all traces now been eliminated from the social interactions of other high-level primates. (Ruse 1986, 227)[1]

To appreciate the connections and similarities that link human morality to the natural animal world, we must examine similarities between human moral behavior and the behavior of other primates; but prior to that, we must reexamine morality itself.

The initial task in considering a broader animal morality is clearing away some of the barriers erected to keep other species from encroaching on the exclusive domain of human morality. Two barriers have been most formidable. The first way of keeping morality the special property of humans has been to make morality a highly rational enterprise. The second, often linked with rationality, has been the claim that morality is *objective*: thus to know moral truth we must have some special knowledge source—Reason, intuition, or divine revelation—that only humans enjoy. The rationality requirement is the subject of this chapter and the next, while moral objectivism is examined in chapter 11.

## Morality and Rationality

Long tradition and philosophical consensus insist that moral behavior requires rational reflection. Philosophers regard that as a common starting point for examinations of morality, a textbook truth that defines moral inquiry.[2] Behavior without moral reflection does not qualify as morally good. A virtuous act must be done deliberatively for the right reasons, and a virtuous life requires reflective development of a virtuous character.

Whatever its philosophical charms, this standard position is misguided. Rational reflection is not necessary for moral behavior. True enough, moral behavior requires a deeper level. If one saves a child from toppling over the ledge, we require further inquiry before judging the act virtuous. If a clumsy would-be murderer was attempting to shove the child off the ledge, the act was vicious. If the rescuer's hand stretched out due to a sudden seizure, the motion is fortunate but not morally significant. If the rescuer was motivated solely by hope of rich reward, then the act loses its positive moral worth. So we must look deeper than the rescuer's extended hand to determine moral worth; but it is motives—rather than reasons—that must be examined, and those motives need not stem from deliberation. If I am a vicious and mercurial but clumsy killer, my spontaneous *non*deliberative attempt to shove you from a ledge is morally vicious though it accidentally saves your life. A mother's spontaneous loving *un*reflective rescue of her child is morally virtuous: if the act is motivated by affection[3] for the child[4] the absence of deliberation does not imply absence of moral worth.

The intent required for moral behavior need not be based on reasons and rules, but neither is it an involuntary reflex. Alan Gewirth ridicules "evolutionary ethics" as based on behavior too crude to be classified as ethical:

> If to be ethical involves intending to act in certain ways that not only benefit other persons besides or in addition to oneself, but also are subject to knowledge, voluntary control, and reasoned choice on the part of the agent, then what evolutionary ethics presents as the content of what it calls ethical behavior is not, in fact, ethical. It is closer to a tropism than to a human action. (Gewirth 1993, 245)

Gewirth's criticism turns on a false dichotomy: acts must be reasoned choices or sink near the level of tropism. But cases of nonrational and nonreflective moral behavior—such as the rescue of a child or friend—are far from being tropistic. They involve intentional behavior that adjusts to changes in circumstances. The nonreflective rescue may involve swimming to the endangered, reaching with a stick, or making an aggressive display to frighten predators; and if the friend should betray trust (or fail to reciprocate), then rather than tropistic repetitions of the rescue behavior, there may be indifference or even attack.[5] The vast space between rational rule-guided reflective behavior and tropism leaves ample room for nonreflective (and nontropistic) intentional moral behavior.[6]

Moral acts such as the rescue of children or friends require the right intent, the proper motive. As we might commonly say, acting virtuously requires acting for the right *reasons*. Unfortunately, that common usage leads into rationalistic temptation. In this context, acting for the right reasons just means acting with the right intentions, and reasoning may have nothing to do with those intentions.

Talk of intentions is another rich source of verbal confusion and rationalistic exaggeration. To act morally I must genuinely *intend* to rescue my child (rather than intend to push the child from a ledge or intend to preserve the lottery ticket clutched in its grubby little fist). Giving a verbal account of that intent is a complicated process; *having* the intent is comparatively simple.

Many animals, human and nonhuman, can form and act upon intentions that they cannot conceptually order and explain. A hyena intends to feed upon an animal carcass, is threatened by a lion (a lion that intends to chase it away), and quickly revises its intentions in favor of safety. A male chimp carefully searches for heavy stones, weighs each in his hand, and selects the heaviest before carrying it some distance to his rival, where—holding the stone as a potential weapon—the chimp begins the long-*intended* intimidation display (de Waal 1989, 39). A subordinate male chimp *intends* to mate with a female, sees the dominant male in the vicinity, and abruptly changes his intentions. Indeed, there are reports of chimps finding their amorous intentions thwarted by the presence of a dominant male and then *intentionally* feigning the intent to forage in another area in order to draw the desired mate out of the dominant's view (de Waal 1982, 48ff.). Such intentional deception is not rare: a subordinate chimp amidst dominants may continue to "search" for food after he has found it, then later return alone to claim the treat (de Waal 1982, 73–74). (The hard-wired reaction of the robin to a dangerous intruder near its nest—the robin limps away from the nest, and since it appears to be easy prey, the predator follows—may be classified as deceptive, but it is certainly not intentional deception; in contrast, the much more variable and flexible deceptive behavior of the chimp does fall under the rubric of intentional.) It is one thing to question the chimp's conceptual apparatus for distinguishing truth from deception; it is quite another—and much simpler—to conclude that the chimp intends to deceive; simpler still to note that the chimp intends to find food, seek cover, threaten a rival, or rescue a friend.

Rather than verbal conceptualization being a necessary condition of specific intentions, it is probably more common for the manifestation of intentions to serve as the prompt for teaching verbal categorizations of intent. Hearing the sound of breaking glass, I rush to the dining room where my child is playing. He is sitting on the floor, next to a crumpled tablecloth that covers some strange bulges.

"What happened?"
"I don't know, Daddy; there was a crash in the kitchen."
"What's under the tablecloth?"
"Oh, nothing."
When I pick up the tablecloth, I discover a broken lamp, and I reprimand my son. "Darling, accidents happen, and I know you didn't mean to pull the tablecloth down and break the lamp. But you shouldn't have tried to deceive me."
"But I wasn't trying to deceive you, Daddy; I was just trying to keep you from finding out that I had broken the lamp."
"But that's what deception *is*: When you told me the crash came from the other room and you hid the broken lamp under the table cloth, you *were* trying to deceive me. You didn't know it was *deception*; but you were intending to mislead me, and that's what it is to intentionally deceive."

In that manner my child may learn to verbally conceptualize and describe intending to deceive; but he needs no instruction in *intending* to deceive: he is quite accomplished at such intentions, long before his verbal categorizations match his devious motives.

Limits to the complex conceptualization of intentions are not confined to children and nonhumans, of course. The defendant in a breaking and entering trial may rightly insist that he did not intend to commit a felony (a necessary condition for being guilty of breaking and entering); all he intended was to break the window and steal the television set.[7] The defendant may lack the conceptual sophistication to intend the commission of a *felony*, yet be fully capable of intending and committing one: by intentionally and knowingly stealing another's property. Likewise, a chimp who is incapable of "intending to act morally" may be quite capable of intending a rescue and thereby *intentionally* performing a morally good act.

Michael Bradie states that "animals can act on the basis of altruistic motives but they do not and cannot form intentions to so act." (Bradie 1994, 136) But in fact animals—humans and nonhumans—can act on, and *intend* to act on, altruistic[8] motives as well as hunger and thirst and concupiscence motives. Other animals may not conceptualize their motives quite as elegantly: they may not *know* they are intending to act altruistically, just as the hapless defendant may not know that he intends to commit a felony. That does not bar them from forming and acting on altruistic intentions. Of course, a chimpanzee cannot intend to perform an altruistic act purely because it is in the category "altruistic"; that is, a chimp cannot resolve to "do a good (altruistic) deed daily." A chimpanzee can, however, be motivated by affection to *intend* the rescue of a friend. When a human performs such an act for identical motives, we count it a moral act, and simple consistency requires the same categorization for chimp altruism.

Humans can, as Bradie insists, form intentions to act altruistically in the strong sense of intending to do an altruistic deed *because* it falls under the *altruistic* classification. Other animals cannot. But that does not preclude other animals performing genuinely altruistic moral acts. In fact, the wonders of (uniquely human) decisions to do altruistic moral acts *because* they are altruistic are greatly exaggerated. Humans do occasionally form such intentions—"I will do a good altruistic deed this day"—though such elaborate moral machinations are rare and exotic exceptions among common everyday moral behavior. And except to Kantians, they are not a source of moral delight and wonderment. "Why did you rescue me?" "What a question; you're my friend; when I saw you in danger, my affection for you immediately prompted me to rush to your rescue." Compare that to: "Why did you rescue me?" "It was an act of altruism; and I always strive to do an altruistic deed daily." The latter may be a moral act; but it is not quintessentially moral, and it is cer-

tainly not moral to the exclusion of the former. Proper intent—
"acting for the right reasons"—is essential for moral behavior;
reasoned deliberation is not.

## Emotional Contagion and Altruism

If a mother—human, chimp, or feline—caresses a distressed and crying infant, she (most commonly) *intends* to comfort it. One might (in the manner of aggressive ethical egoists)
disparage such comforting as merely relieving oneself of the discomfort caused by the infant's crying. For example:

> Chimpanzees show patterns of behavior that appear, from a
> psychological perspective, only weakly altruistic. Much of what
> might qualify as chimpanzee altruism may be based on the
> arousal of feelings of emotional distress in the helper, perhaps
> through emotional contagion, and the role of social attribution
> is unclear when helping is prompted by emotional contagion.
> (Povinelli and Godfrey 1993, 310)

But while "feelings of distress" may certainly be aroused in the
mother, it is still generally the case that the mother genuinely
intends to relieve the infant's distress. Were her motive only the
relief of her own "emotional contagion" discomfort, the purpose
might be achieved more readily by moving out of earshot or
tossing the infant from a high branch.

Given the ease of escape from "the emotional contagion" of
distress, it is hardly plausible that "apparent altruism" is
caused by the "altruistic" helper's self-interest in reducing his
or her own suffering. But just as it is invoked by Povinelli and
Godfrey to explain away "chimpanzee altruism," so also it has
been a favorite psychological explanation for apparent acts of
human altruism. Social psychologists call this the "aversive-
arousal reduction" account of altruism: a sufferer arouses aversive feelings among those nearby, and in order to reduce their
own aroused discomfort they attempt to aid the sufferer. Such
aid is (as Batson 1991, 43ff. characterizes it) more "pseudoaltruistic" than genuinely altruistic, since the motive of the aid-
giver is relief of his or her own distress (when such reduction of
aversive stimuli is most conveniently achieved by giving aid).

In a series of cleverly designed experiments, Daniel Batson
has demonstrated the implausibility of the popular aversive-

arousal reduction account of "altruism." Batson and other researchers have shown that the behavior *predicted* by the aversive-arousal reduction hypothesis simply does not occur. For example, if the aversive-arousal reduction hypothesis were correct, then when escape behavior becomes increasingly easy (escape is one way of reducing the supposed aversive arousal from another's suffering) subjects should help less and escape more. But in fact ease of escape has no influence on willingness to help another in distress (Batson 1991, 109–127).

So the aversive-arousal reduction hypothesis fails to account for the altruistic behavior of animals, including human animals. But the fact that it is so readily embraced as an explanation is significant in its own right, for it reveals a good deal about some insidiously influential assumptions. Suppose that I am suffering, and that my suffering makes you feel bad (through "emotional contagion"); it need not follow that your efforts to relieve my suffering are directed exclusively at the reduction of your own suffering. That may be one of your motives; but another motive—alongside the first, and not in conflict with the first, nor lessened nor cheapened nor "pseudofied" due to the presence of the first—may be the genuinely altruistic motive of relieving *my* suffering. Indeed, it should be rather surprising if in most instances altruistic behavior were motivated *purely* by either such motive, rather than a combination of the two. Why should there be such a tendency—among philosophers, and even among some social psychologists—to draw such a radical distinction between them? The motive of the social psychologist may be innocent enough: setting up artificial distinctions may be necessary in order to test competing hypotheses. But why should philosophers assume that being motivated by "emotional contagion" *excludes* the influence of genuine altruism? Lurking in the philosophical shadows is the ghost of Kant. Only from a Kantian assumption that a genuinely moral act must be done *purely* for duty (and not at all from inclination) could it seem that a genuine act of altruistic virtue is fatally contaminated by any taint of pleasure or pain reduction or inclination for oneself.

The Kantian view is designed to set moral behavior—particularly rule-governed, duty-driven, human rational moral behavior—securely apart from the natural world. But other than the dubious benefit of securing for humanity a special godlike sphere *apart* from other animals, such a moral view has little to recommend it. As already noted, if your motive in rescuing me is purely to perform a dutiful deed, then I may be glad of being rescued, but I shall hardly regard your motives as purer or nobler or more virtuous than the motives of one who rushes to my rescue from immediate affection and heartfelt concern for my welfare, with no dutiful deliberations entering into it.

There is a competitor to the Kantian moral tradition that is more easily accommodated into the natural world and the actual behavior of humans and other animals: to be virtuous is to be moved by the right sorts of concerns and affections and revulsions. One who takes genuine delight in the pleasures of others and feels deep sympathy with the sufferings of others is a Kantian moral cipher, but perhaps an Aristotelian moral hero. If you rescue me or feed me or house me because it would cause you great sorrow to know that I am suffering, that need not be a "pseudoaltruistic" motive: you are genuinely aiming to relieve *my* suffering. Likewise, if making others happy is a source of genuine joy for you, then you are still striving to make *others* happy. That your activities also bring you joy does not mean that you are primarily seeking your own selfish pleasure, nor does it lessen your genuine striving for the happiness of others. Playing tennis makes me happy; but I don't play tennis in order to be happy: I play tennis because I want to play tennis. If you offered me the happiness, but without the bother of playing tennis, I should think that no bargain. Likewise, a virtuous person who is made happy by bringing joy to others is acting altruistically (not pseudoaltruistically); and if she were offered the experience of joy—perhaps through some Nozickian pleasure machine—but without the bother of helping others, she would find it a poor and detestable offer. She takes great joy in helping others; but she does not help others in order to make herself joyful. (Of course should she become depressed, and her kind acts no longer bring her any pleasure, her kind behavior might eventually extinguish; but the fact that her pleasure holds her altruistic behavior steadily in force does *not* imply that her altruism is actually aimed at her own pleasure.)

## Moral Individualism vs. Natural Sympathy

The Kantian requirement of acting purely from duty is linked with another problematic Kantian principle: rugged moral individualism. Each of us is a distinct autonomous individual lawgiver. As legislators of our own sublime universal moral law, we are self-contained and self-sufficient. Needing the support or sympathy or affection of others is a sign of weakness. Even the feeling of sympathy or empathy toward others undermines the worth of acting purely from the demands of rational duty imposed upon oneself by force of one's own splendidly isolated will. From such a perspective, altruism is amazing, prompting awe in equal measure for "the starry heavens above me and the moral law within me" (Kant 1788/1949, 259). But humans, like other social animals, were never rugged individuals who gathered together as independent monads to draw up a social contract; nor are humans morally or psychologically self-sufficient lawgivers who enter moral deliberations as gloriously independent entities. Mutual sympathy is a common and vital moral element among humans, and the detached purely nonsympathetic moral lawgiver is more likely a sociopath than a saint. Like many other animals, we feel genuine concern and sympathy for others. We are touched by their sufferings and moved to alleviate their pain. Along with that, we may feel personal sympathetic distress at their suffering, but our efforts are nonetheless aimed at the good of others rather than exclusively our own comfort. The Kantian assumption of moral individualism imposes an artificial problem: How can we account for altruistic behavior toward other individuals with whom we have no essential connection? The answer requires the awesome and uniquely human powers of the rational moral will, and so only humans can be moral actors.

If reason and duty-following and deliberation are required for genuine altruism, then that is a way of keeping altruism—and any moral behavior associated with it—the exclusive property of humans. But that is not a plausible approach to human altruism; and recognizing the existence of genuine altruism in nonrational (and nonhuman) behavior helps to free our moral perspective from a stiflingly narrow range of vision.

For those who still insist that the human parent's spontaneous rescues are deliberative and thus categorically—and morally—different from those of other species, then the burden of establishing that difference will not be a small one. One might claim that the apparently similar acts of the human parent are significantly different because the human deliberates: not consciously, but subconsciously. But since the evidence for such subconscious deliberation is merely the human status of the actor, the claim seems no better than question begging. No doubt we have a richer conceptual range for considering our friends and rivals and offspring, a conceptual map that outstrips that enjoyed by chimp, monkey, and mouse. But in the case of nondeliberative spontaneous rescue, those conceptual differences do not come into play. Nor will it help to suggest that the *moral* individual's spontaneous acts must be in *accord* with a morality she has reflectively approved. In Jonathan Bennett's example (Bennett 1974), Huck Finn's affection for Jim moves him to act morally by hiding Jim from the slavers, but Huck does not follow any previously approved moral code. To the contrary, Huck's morally good act is in direct conflict with the only moral code he considers and recognizes.

Imagine a hungry individual who can secure food only by inflicting pain on one of her fellows. If she refrains from taking the desired food, then she is acting morally. Or so we would say, if she were a member of our species. When we discover that she is a rhesus monkey, the behavior is pushed out of the moral realm.[9] Such implausible categorizations tie our understanding of morality in knots. The rhesus monkey does not act from rational reflection on the demands of duty, but such a standard excludes a broad range of almost paradigmatic moral behavior. By that standard, the mother who risks her life to save her child—spontaneously and without hesitation or deliberation—does not act morally. But so far from refusing to consider such nondeliberative spontaneous acts of altruistic care as moral, in many instances the moral lustre is tarnished if deliberation intervenes. If after deliberative consideration of your duty, you rescue me from my precarious place on the cliff's edge, then I shall be glad of your moral character and acts. But I shall be more impressed by your virtue if you spontaneously throw yourself into my rescue.[10] "Why did you risk your life to save the children from the burning building?" "I heard the screams, considered what I should do, and decided that it was my duty to attempt a rescue." "I heard the screams and immediately felt I had to rescue the children. Reflections on duty had nothing to do with it." The former may be virtuous, but not more virtuous than the latter.[11]

## The Development of Moral Character

There are good reasons, both biological and philosophical, for denying that specific moral acts require rational reflection.

But there remains a deeper question (and a deeper objection) to answer: Does moral *character* require rational reflection? Joyce gives bread to a hungry child, acting from generous motives. She feels affection and concern for the child and wishes to relieve the child's hunger. It still does not follow (so the objection goes) that Joyce is acting virtuously. Before her behavior and character can be morally evaluated it must be scrutinized more closely, with attention to its causal history.

Joyce is generous and compassionate, true enough; but how did she become so? Was she merely lucky to be born with a generous and compassionate nature? If so (the objection continues), that calls her apparently virtuous acts into question, since they do not stem from a genuinely virtuous character. Joyce's happen-chance generosity is the result of her fortunate disposition, and that is too shallow a foundation for moral character. If she is merely acting from inclination, then we may be pleased that she acts generously, but she is no more virtuous than is the capricious wind virtuous when it blows a crust toward a hungry child. Or perhaps Joyce is generous because she had the good fortune to be shaped by a generous and well-ordered society. Joyce now acts generously, and does so from her own generous inclination; but that is not enough for genuine virtue, since (on this line of objection) her character is just the conditioned product of the society in which she was lucky to be born. Had she been born into a vicious culture, she would have a vicious character. Joyce is good-hearted and generous, but she is not really virtuous. She is morally lucky, not morally good.

This line of argument claims that genuine moral character requires something deeper than mere acquiescence to inclinations or culture. It requires the deliberate reflective considered choice of the character one favors, the higher-level approval of one's inclinations and commitments. Without such reflective commitment one may, like the wind, blow well or ill; but one cannot be moral nor act morally. Thus even if it is possible for a particular spontaneous act to be genuinely moral, that can occur only when the act is the product of a reflective moral life. Morality may not require constant rational reflection, but rational reflection is a requisite foundation.

Or so the argument goes. But on closer examination, this claim that morality requires reflection also fails. If Joyce gives bread to a hungry child or extends her hand in rescue, her motive may be generous and her act virtous though she has not reflected upon it; and in like manner, Joyce's character may encompass a profound and steadfast commitment to feeding the hungry and rescuing the endangered even though she has never reflectively examined nor deliberately adopted her commitments.[12] Profound commitments and enduring characters are not exclusively (nor even typically) the product of rational reflection.[13] To suppose that such nonreflective commitments must be superficial or transitory or spurious is to grossly over-intellectualize the development of character. Joyce's profound love for her children may be resolute and enduring and nonreflective. And just as there might be grounds for questioning the moral virtue of someone who must call duty to mind before acting to rescue an endangered child, likewise one might be less confident of the steadfast virtuous character of an individual who requires reflection to reach such basic moral commitments as care for the unfortunate. Sonya concludes after rational reflection that she must commit to caring for the unfortunate; she may be virtuous, but it is hardly obvious that she is more virtuous—or more reliably and sustainably and deeply virtuous—than is Joyce, who embraces caring for the unfortunate as an immediate and basic value requiring neither rational reflection nor justification.

Still, one may be troubled by the possibility that the profoundly virtuous individual isn't really virtuous: she is only lucky to have good deep durable inclinations, and she cannot be truly virtuous since she did not reflectively choose her character. This objection to any biological or evolutionary contribution to morality is voiced by Patricia Williams. She claims that it is impossible to develop "theories of prescriptive evolved ethics which do not suffer from internal, logical contradictions" (Williams 1993, 238). The reason for such inescapable incoherence is that "the minimum requirement for beings to be ethical is that they can legitimately be blamed, praised, and held responsible for their actions," and "in order to deserve praise or blame or to be held responsible for their actions" beings "must be able to self-reflect," they "must be able to weigh and deliberate among various options," and they must be able to make and act on choices based on such deliberations (Williams 1993, 234).

Obviously this leaves those incapable of higher-order rational reflection outside the moral realm and calls into question the virtuous character of nonreflective Joyce. But Williams's argument turns on a basic confusion between requirements for being *moral* and requirements for being morally *responsible*. Joyce is generous and compassionate. She cares for the hungry, rescues the imperilled, and struggles against injustice; and she does so from pure motives—she is concerned for the unfortunate and wants their suffering to end, and she seeks neither fame nor fortune nor even treasure in heaven (nor merely relief from "aroused distress"). But why is Joyce so compassionate and generous and virtuous? That is a different and difficult question. Perhaps she is genetically predisposed to generosity, or enjoyed a good moral upbringing, or some combination of the two. Or maybe it stems from philosophical study and reflection, that led her to a deep rational commitment to principles of duty toward the unfortunate. Possibly it was a religious conversion experience, the gift of God's grace and not of Joyce's work. It doesn't matter. Whatever the causal source, Joyce is morally virtuous: she acts virtuously, from virtuous motives, through a virtuous character. Whether the causes are God, nature, or nurture does not affect the fact that she is genuinely virtuous.

But it does affect our judgment of whether she is morally *responsible* for being profoundly virtuous. If Joyce is virtuous because she has generous genes, then she is virtuous by genetic luck; if because of a good social upbringing, she is lucky in her early environment, but again she is not morally responsible for her fortunate virtue.[14] If Joyce is to be not only virtuous, but also morally responsible for her good character and acts, then something more is needed. A favorite philosophical candidate (as championed by Kant and adopted by Patricia Williams) is rational reflection and deliberative choice. Thus for Kant, generous inclinations count nothing toward virtue, since one's endowment of generous inclination is a matter of fortune. Following the stern rational dictates of duty—without regard to inclinations, ideally in opposition to them—sets one apart from the natural world and establishes autonomy and moral responsibility. By my lights, such a view is implausible; but whatever the merits of that Kantian approach, the important point here is that the rational deliberation is designed to save moral *responsibility* rather than moral behavior or moral character. If Joyce is virtuous because of her fortunate childhood training, then she is not morally responsible for being virtuous; she may be virtuous, nonetheless.

Rational reflection figures prominently in recent efforts to save moral responsibility. According to Harry G. Frankfurt (1969, 1971) and Gerald Dworkin (1988), Joyce is not morally responsible for her desire to feed the hungry nor her desire to take drugs; she is, however, morally responsible for reflecting upon those desires and for her reflective decision concerning her higher-order evaluations: is this a desire I wish to have, the person I wish to be. The argument of the previous chapters was that rational reflection could not support moral responsibility; but whatever the verdict on whether such higher-order reflection is either necessary or sufficient for moral responsibility, that question is a different one from the question of whether rational reflection is necessary for moral behavior and moral character.[15] In short, even if one supposes that rational higher-order reflection is essential for moral *responsibility*, it does not follow that morality—including moral acts and moral character—requires rational reflection.[16]

The conclusion is that reason is not required for morality. But that is not to suggest that reason must be banished from moral life, leaving only spontaneous nonreflective acts as genuinely moral. Morality is not built on a foundation of reason, but reasoned reflection and inquiry can make valuable contributions to our moral lives. The nonrational *basis* of morality and the reasoned *enhancement* of morality are the subject of the next chapter.

# 10

---

## What Reason Adds
## to Animal Morality

The previous chapter argued that rational reflection is not necessary for morality, and biological inquiry into the development of moral behavior gives further support to that conclusion. Rather than higher intelligence being a condition of morality, it is more likely that the conditions are reversed. Our rational faculties developed to enhance and extend moral sentiments of affection and concern,[1] rather than moral concern and moral behavior emerging from higher intellectual (social-contract following)[2] capacities.

The biological roots of other-regarding behavior are in kin altruism. The solicitous care a parent bestows upon its offspring, the concern shown for a sibling: these are easily explained in terms of their survival enhancement of the individual's genes. Animals that protect and nurture their offspring are more likely to preserve replicas of their genes, including any genetic tendency toward kin altruism. To move beyond regard for close kin requires the resources of reciprocal altruism. Reciprocal altruism—in which generous behavior is given and reciprocated—can be found in a number of species, including humans. A monkey removes parasites from the back of another, and the kindness is reciprocated. A human rubs suntan lotion on a companion's back, and the favor is returned. Reciprocal altruism is certainly advantageous, but it is not obvious how it might have been initiated. As James Rachels (following Darwin's suggestions) describes the process:

> This might at first be a simple thing: A and B both have parasites that are hard to reach, and they both want them

113

removed; in casting about for a way to accomplish this, A removes B's parasite and then presents himself, in a suggestive posture, to B; B "catches on" to the game, and sees that his own welfare is being served by playing this game of tit-for-tat, so B then removes A's parasite. (1990, 157)

As Rachels notes, this process requires considerable intelligence:

It is significant that all the most impressive examples of non-kin altruism are from the so-called "higher" animals—humans, monkeys, baboons, and so on—animals in which the power of reasoning is well developed. In the "lower" animals we find only kin altruism. This seems to confirm Darwin's speculation that the development of general altruism might go hand-in-hand with the development of intelligence. (1990, 157)

This is a plausible account, but we should not exaggerate the intelligence involved. Such reciprocal altruism does not require the drawing up of contracts, nor even conceptualization of the nature of the relationship. Basically it requires the capacity to distinguish among individuals and recognize and remember requests and bequests of reciprocal kindness.

For reciprocal altruism to flourish, animals had to make increasingly subtle distinctions: Is this a fellow who will reciprocate my altruistic acts? Is this an individual to whom I "owe a favor"? The extension of reciprocal altruism—and the extension of cooperative morality—encourages the development of intelligence, rather than higher intelligence clearing the way for morality. Or they develop together. Either way, the myth of morality awaiting the development of higher intelligence (and thus morality requiring rational reflection) is a distortion.

Richard Alexander offers a simple but plausible account of how morality might develop in conjunction with development of higher intelligence. According to Alexander, altruism starts at home, with kin-altruism and later reciprocal altruism. Cooperative behavior (and thus a disposition for cooperative behavior) toward reciprocators (and kin) is beneficial, and flourishes. Cooperating with shirkers or deceivers is not beneficial, and so along with extended cooperative behavior, there must evolve improved cognitive abilities to detect the noncooperative. As such capacities strengthen, the advantages of being a sincerely generous cooperator become enhanced, and the advantages of being a genuinely generous and noncalculating giver and reciprocator increase. As Alexander notes:

> . . . in most social circumstances the chance to pay someone back (for either helping or not helping), and to avoid him or seek him out for establishing a reciprocal realtionship if it were not actually you he was helping, are multiple and extend across long periods. If he were careful enough to assess his costs in the *immediate situation* (hence, seemed to be acting like a cynical cost-benefit assessor who contemplates the effects of each act upon his own interests), then astute observers would avoid him in future interactions in favor of others more likely to be more beneficent or less careful about their own or immediate self-interests, and he could lose mightily on that account. Also, he could err and fail to help when he should have on other grounds. In either case his tendency to be a conscious, deliberate, cynical, cost-benefit tester in each circumstance would cause him to lose. On the other hand, if he occasionally erred in the specific situation on the side of beneficence this would label him as a good interactant to seek out, and one to whom help could be given with little fear of being short-changed. (Alexander 1987, 119)

And of course the best and most efficient way to give the impression of being a noncalculating generous and willing reciprocator is to actually possess beneficent and generous dispositions. Thus cooperative behavior evolved from rudimentary reciprocal processes, and detection of shirkers (and the cognitive capacities required for that task) evolved along with the development of altruistic cooperation.[3]

The view that genuine cooperative dispositions and principled commitment to cooperative altruism developed out of cruder, more rudimentary forms of altruism (such as kin and reciprocal altruism) has recently been criticized by Neven Sesardic. He considers the possibility that "our reason in its ascent to the completely generalized altruism" might work from cruder, limited forms of altruism that are developed further by means of rules and principles; and Sesardic dismisses the possibility as a nonstarter. He argues that:

> . . . psychological altruism toward relatives can be a purely Darwinian product. What remains highly dubious, however, is whether this kind of incipient nonegoism could serve as a

foothold for our reason in its ascent to the completely generalized altruism. If we want to justify rationally the normative
standpoint of universal altruism this surely cannot be
achieved by relying solely on the purely factual premise that
humans already display a kind of selective altruism. Those
philosophers who want to claim that it is our reason that helps
us to cross the border between the narrow-scope altruism and
principled altruism are under obligation . . . to show . . . that
this initial, minimal altruism is itself rationally justified. This
is necessary simply because reason cannot generalize something on the ground that it exists, but only on the ground that
it is reasonable in the first place. Therefore the cognitivist
argument . . . cannot bootstrap itself by appealing to the factual premise that evolutionary forces have produced one kind
of altruism [Sesardic's designation for an altruism of intention
to benefit others at one's own expense], in the hope that it has
then only to proceed further and broaden the scope of this
other-benefiting behavioral tendency. No, reason has to take
the uphill path and develop the rational defense of altruism all
the way from the very beginning. (Sesardic 1995, 147)

If we require a complete rational justification for altruism,
then indeed that will require "the rational defense of altruism all
the way from the very beginning"; and such an account is
unlikely in any case, but particularly unlikely to be built upon
simple kin or reciprocal inclinations of cooperation or generosity.[4] But if reason is called on for more modest enterprises, it
may have more success. We do not need (and, in my view, could
not have) a rational justification for our most basic inclinations
toward cooperation and generosity. We simply have them, and
are glad we have them, and it is possible to give a plausible biological account of why we have them. Reason cannot offer a
"deep foundational justification" of altruism. Instead (as will be
discussed in the next section) reason is a special means of
enhancing and enlarging altruism. That the rational enhancement does not require "reason all the way down" is easily illus-
trated. I feel generous altruistic and cooperative motives toward
my family and my friends: motives that are deep and genuine,
but not rationally founded. Reason may push me to extend
those altruistic dispositions: I care for (friend or relative)
Martha; Martha is in relevant respects similar to Nancy; therefore to be consistent, I should extend my concern and care to
Nancy, as well. The power of such rational extensions of altruistic dispositions should not be exaggerated; but whatever their

effectiveness, they do not require that the basic altruistic moral motivations be rationally grounded. Again, I may use rules and principles to strengthen and sustain my generous impulses toward my children, but such rational strengthening does not require rationality all the way down: we do not (thankfully) require good reasons or reflective rationality in order to love our children.

## What Reason Adds to Animal Morality

Morality does not require reason, but reason is not cast out of morality. Morality can and does exist without higher rule-following reflective intelligence. Nonetheless, higher intelligence offers special capacities for the enhancement of morality.[5]

We are medical researchers, eager to test a very promising (but potentially dangerous) cancer drug on human subjects. Of course we shall seek "informed consent" from all the experimental subjects; but who will be (morally) the best experimental subjects? Without giving it much thought, we may assume that the sickest and the least productive should be selected: they contribute little to society; and since they are already unlikely to recover, there is less to lose if the experimental drug proves harmful. But Hans Jonas (1969) argues that such an approach is a temptation to be avoided, since it makes those who are most vulnerable into experimental objects that are used for the purposes and benefit of others. We should instead seek experimental subjects who are strongest and healthiest and most intelligent, for they are not only least vulnerable but also are more likely to share the goals of the research and thus not be turned into pawns for projects in which they have no genuine interest. Such rational reflection is valuable: it can make us acutely aware of basic moral inclinations and principles that had been obscured by the press of immediate interests and circumstances. (Notice that Jonas does not give arguments for why it is morally right to protect those who are particularly vulnerable. At that level, we are dealing with basic moral inclinations that are not a product of reason. If one lacks such protective inclinations—for example, if one is pushed by basic predatory motives toward exploitation of the weak—then Jonas's reasoned argument cannot get started.)

That is a case in which rational reflection sharpens and

focuses our moral inclinations (in this case, our inclinations toward protecting the weak and helpless). But reason can also be used to strengthen and extend our basic moral inclinations and affections. Consider Huck Finn. As Jonathan Bennett notes, even in the absence of aid from moral principle—indeed, when his moral principles are a moral impediment—Huck manages to act morally, motivated by sympathy for his friend Jim. Huck without sound moral principles is morally good, but Huck with sound moral principles would be morally better. To see why, we need only imagine a less appealing Jim: short-tempered, arrogant, and selfish. It would have been morally wrong to betray such a repellent person to the slavers, but it is doubtful that Huck's sympathies would have done the trick. In such circumstances—when sympathies have worn thin, the going is rougher, and affection fails in force or range—deliberative efforts and rational reflection on rules can enhance and strengthen and sustain moral behavior.[6]

Our inclinations to altruism and kindness are natural and deep, but they are hardly boundless. Love and concern prompt me to awaken and calm my child's nightmarish fears, and the dictates of duty do not enter into it. (One who must be prodded by duty to act generously toward a child is morally deficient rather than morally exemplary.) Of course I wish to stay in my warm bed, but not nearly so much as I wish to rush to the side of my terrified child. I rush with almost equal inclination to the aid of my nieces and nephews, and to a lesser but still-considerable degree to the aid of distressed members of my community. But there are limits: my desire to help those across the sea is still weaker, and I may need to reflect upon rules of duty to extend my concern. Also, if my child "exhausts my patience," then duty may reinforce my failing sympathies. But rather than a break from inclinations, this use of duty extends and strengthens them.

What can a rule-system of duties do that natural inclination cannot? Most dramatic is the extension of concern—through demands of rational consistency and universalization—beyond our immediate inclinations to help family and friends. But the benefits of rule-based sympathy enhancement begin at home. When (through exhaustion or extinction or frustration) my warm sympathies for family and friends run low, I can turn to duties and rules to reaffirm my commitments and thus take steps to restore my natural inclinations of care and concern. Use of such rules is a special enhancement and strengthener; but it is not unlike other special acts made possible by greater intelligence, such as reflecting upon past kindnesses to rekindle warm feelings of kinship and affection. When despondent Diana returns Carmen's kindness with sullen indifference, Carmen can consider principles—such as "Love is not love that alters when it alteration finds"—she has learned to treasure, principles that may sustain her generous affection through periods when it is not immediately advantageous. And Carmen can reflect with satisfaction upon her own generous behavior to preserve and strengthen it. Or Carmen may recall a kind and consoling letter received from Diana after a misfortune. Thus Carmen has special reflective resources (including but not limited to reflections on rules of duty) to strengthen and sustain and enlarge sympathies, resources that animals of lesser intelligence cannot employ. Reasoned adherence to rules of duty is a special enhancement of sympathetic inclinations, but the enhancements are built on basic moral sympathies that retain their moral status.[7]

Carmen can reflect upon rules to sustain her affection, and she can also employ rules and reflection to strengthen the character she wants and values. Carmen is strongly inclined toward trusting and supportive relations with others: she values such cooperative friendship. But she is also pulled toward greed, which threatens her friendly relations. If she values friendship more than acquisitiveness, then Carmen may avoid situations in which her greed dominates and maximize situations in which friendship keeps greed in check. This process may happen without Carmen being aware of it, and certainly without any reflection or deliberation; but it may also occur by design: Carmen might recognize that she values friendship over greed and deliberately choose to strengthen her cooperative nonselfish behavior, perhaps by adopting a rule to "share good fortune with friends and resist the temptations of greed." Such rule-following and second-order reflection is often an effective means of strengthening valued behavior, and its utility should be appreciated and perhaps celebrated; but it need not (the more common philosophical danger) be exaggerated.[8]

Second-order reflection is a valuable and uniquely human means of shaping and enhancing behavior and character, but it is best understood as a further means of moral development rather than the defining feature of genuine moral activity. Mary

Midgley seems to limit genuine moral acts to those animals (all of them humans) with the high level of reflective self-awareness to facilitate "the effort to reinforce or reshape one's central character by forming a constant framework of decision adapted to it, the effort to establish lasting policies with which incoming impulses can agree or conflict" (1994, 174–175). But second-order reflection on rules and "policies" is only one means of moral development, and probably not the most effective (though it takes the prize for most sophisticated). Moral development occurs—and occurs intentionally—without such second-order reflection. I strongly value acting generously toward my friends and take steps to intentionally achieve that end. I may do so without reflecting on whether I *also* value (at a second-order level) *wanting* to be the sort of individual who favors friendship over greed. Second-order reflection is a useful means of enhancing moral behavior, but it is not the only means, and in any case the moral behavior it enhances can exist prior to and in the absence of such higher-order reflectiveness. If I don't reflect on the past (as a "man of action," my credo is "Don't cry over spilt milk," or perhaps "Let the dead bury the dead"), I may still act in ways that are profoundly virtuous or vicious, from established and enduring sympathies.

Rules and reason and reflection are not necessary for moral character and moral behavior, though they are no less valuable for moral development. With that in mind, we can effectively consider the genuine moral importance of reflecting on past behavior. Darwin regarded such reflection (with the aid of the enduring "social instincts") as the source of conscience and an important element in the potential reform of character:

> At the moment of action, man will no doubt be apt to follow the stronger impulse [of hunger or vengeance or danger-avoidance, often at the expense of his fellows]; and though this may occasionally prompt him to the noblest deeds, it will far more commonly lead him to gratify his own desires at the expense of other men. But after their gratification, when past and weaker impressions are contrasted with the [comparatively weak but] ever-enduring social instincts, retribution will surely come. Man will then feel dissatisfaction with himself, and will resolve with more or less force to act differently in the future. This is conscience; for conscience looks backwards and judges past actions, inducing that kind of dissatisfaction, which if weak we call regret, and if severe remorse. (Darwin, 1871, 90)

Thus reflection (including reflection on the past) is a valuable resource for enhancing moral behavior. Darwin even rates it a special distinctive feature of humans:

> Why does man regret, even though he may endeavour to banish any such regret, that he has followed the one natural impulse, rather than the other; and why does he further feel that he ought to regret his conduct? Man in this respect differs profoundly from the lower animals. (Darwin 1871, 89)

Reflective humans thus have the potential for doing *better* at morality, and this is an important advance; it does not follow that we are the only moral animals. The differences may be profound, but not nearly that profound.

I may not realize that I am acting morally (or immorally) without some degree of higher-order reflection, and perhaps I shall feel no shame in my immorality nor pride in my good character without such higher-order reflectiveness (though such claims are certainly open to question). But even if the absence of second-order reflection should imply restrictions on my moral awareness, I can still intentionally act morally or immorally and be profoundly virtuous or vicious. One might suggest that only through higher-order reflection could one be really committed to either a virtuous or vicious path; but that line of argument has already been rejected (the nonreflective but steadfastly loyal friend is sufficient counterexameple to such overrationalizing of moral commitment). In short, higher-order reflectiveness and the deliberate use of rules is a special way of strengthening moral behavior and character, but similar effects can be gained without such higher-order reflection. If moral behavior enhanced by second-order reflectiveness is granted exclusive title to morality, then the full rich range of moral development and functioning will be obscured.

When rule-following is recognized as an *enhancement* of moral behavior (and not given exclusive title to morality), many of the concerns of those who emphasize moral rule-following can still be accommodated. For example, Elliott Sober emphasizes:

> . . . highlighting one aspect of morality that strikes me as very important, which is glossed over when one equates morality and altruism. This is the *impersonality* of moral rules. By this

> I mean that people generally recognize that what is right for
> them to do is right for anyone else to do who is similarly situ-
> ated. (Sober 1993, 212–213)

That is an important element in developing and sustaining
morality: it keeps morality on a steadier and sturdier course
than can be achieved exclusively through the moral resources
of sympathy and immediate concern. But it is an important
enhancement that is made possible by the marvelous adaptive
powers of human reason, rather than a defining necessary condition of moral behavior. Sober is right to counsel against
neglecting or "glossing over" the importance of such imperson-
ality; but among philosophers, that is hardly a danger. The
problem is more likely to be that this important moral enhancement—of which humans are uniquely capable—will draw so
much attention (and Kantian "awe") that the basic moral core
that we share with other species is ignored or disparaged.

As Lawrence Blum has noted (1980, 77–89), insisting that
all moral behavior must be based on impartial principles of uni-
versalizability will rule much altruistic behavior out of the realm
of morality—to the impoverishment of our moral lives and our
*mis*understanding of morality. Blum gives the following example:

> . . . if an Italian is dedicated to helping poor Italians, and is
> genuinely concerned about their welfare, then, even if he
> would not be so concerned if the persons were not Italians, he
> is still concerned genuinely for them for their own sakes; and,
> on my view, that attitude (and the actions stemming from it)
> have moral value. (Blum 1980, 79)

Of course (as Blum notes) if this concern for Italians is linked
with hatred for non-Italians, then certainly the individual is in
that respect morally deficient; and if the concern for Italians is
really just a way of expressing contempt for all non-Italians, then
the attitude is morally loathsome. But such negative aspects
need not be part of the individual's view. As Blum notes:

> A person may be deeply devoted to the welfare of the Italian
> community without being suspicious of, or wishing the harm
> of, non-Italians. He may even wish well for non-Italian com-
> munities and recognize the worthiness of their aspirations,
> though he does not have the actual concern for them which he
> has for his own community. (1980, 80)

Reasons and rules and universalizing can extend concern, and that is a valuable element of moral development. But celebrating the importance of such rational moral universalizing does not require that we ignore or disparage—or exclude from moral recognition—more limited, nonuniversalized moral concerns based on altruistic emotions and concerns. Blum states the position clearly:

> It is important to recognize that genuine devotion to a particular group—family, neighborhood, ethnic community, ethnic group, club—is in itself morally good, and becomes morally suspect only when it involves a deficient stance toward others [when the affection for Italians is clouded by contempt for non-Italians]. It is morally good in that it involves (among other things) an admirable degree of sympathy, compassion, and concern for others. Moral philosophy ought to be able to give expression to the moral value of such an attitude, and an exclusively universalist perspective cannot do so. (Blum 1980, 80)

The rational universalizing process is a wonderful enhancement and extension of moral concern, but more limited affection-based moral concern should not be treated as some amoral or "protomoral" stage that can be shoved aside now that we have reached the pinnacle of universalized rationalistic duty-following morality. The animal—whether human or otherwise—whose moral concern does not extend beyond the members of his or her community has a limited moral scope, but is still capable of genuine moral behavior. If rational impersonal universalization were a necessary condition for morality, then morality would be a narrow and exclusive realm indeed: after all, even the most dedicated universalizers among humans have traditionally failed to extend their concerns beyond the community of their own species. But such speciesism, regrettable as it may be, does not render their human-limited moral concerns null and void.

## The Alliance of Duty and Affection

Reason and rule-following enhance autonomy. They open more paths and possibilities, and reflective reason is thus a valuable adaptation. But it offers an enhancement of animal autonomy, just as keener scent and swifter feet also enhance autonomy. Higher reason does not give human animals exclusive title to autonomy: autonomy enhanced by human intelligence is an extension and development of a much broader animal autonomy. Likewise, moral behavior—and moral affections—are enhanced by the special human adaptation of hierarchical reflection and rule-following; but this enhancement is not the origin of morality, and it is an enhancement, rather than a competitor, to affection-based morality.

Reasoned morality is an ally—rather than an adversary— to morality rooted in animal affections; but the deep traditional divide between moral humans and all other animals has obscured this cooperative relation. Even some who have been most perceptive in recognizing and celebrating affection-based morality have tended to see reason-based, rule-following morality as a competitor. For example, Lawrence Blum (1980) develops an enlightening account of the genuinely *moral* dimension of altruistic emotions, noting that such emotions focus our concern on "the weal and the woe" of others and motivate moral feelings and moral behavior on their behalf. He argues that such motives are genuinely moral and inherently valuable and that philosophers have long ignored or undervalued them in favor of moral acts done from dutiful rational reflection. But Blum attempts to carve out a moral space for such nonreflective sympathetically motivated acts by *adding* a new wing to the edifice of morality. Reflective duty morality stays in its accustomed place, and altruistic affection and sympathy operate in a separate area of our moral lives:

> Generally, the sense of duty and the altruistic emotions operate in different, if sometimes overlapping, areas of our lives. . . .
> But the kind man does not do the same things the conscientious man does. These two virtues work in different areas of our lives. . . . Actions (responses) expressive of sympathy convey goods which acts motivated by duty do not. (1980, 165, 167)

Certainly sympathy can convey goods (such as the goods of personal concern and affection) that duty cannot; but the connection is closer than Blum suggests. On Blum's model, duty emerges as an exalted kind of human moral capacity, with little connection to moral sympathies (though the areas in which they operate may overlap, they function independently of one another). But in fact their connections run deeper. Rational duty morality did not originate in remarkable reflective powers that transcend our altruistic sympathies. The rules of duty developed to enhance and extend and sustain the moral motives of sympathy and altruism from which morality developed, and duty often contributes in precisely the situations where moral altruistic emotions also operate: my kindness to my child or my friend generally is fueled by altruistic emotions of affection, but when such motivation runs low, duty can sustain my generous behavior. Even for cases in which the differences are most marked—my kindness to a stranger is typically motivated by duty, in contrast to the altruistic affection that motivates kindness to my children—the development of duty is best viewed as a special extension and widening of the behavior motivated by affections. When this close connection is recognized, there is less temptation to draw invidious comparisons between them. It is not a question of which moral motive—affection or duty—is preferable, for they work best together.

There is not a forced choice between the sympathetic biological roots and the deliberative enhancement of ethics. The deliberative enhancement (including second-order reflection) is important; but it is no more a transcending of the sympathetic roots than enhanced eyesight is a transcending of the other senses. The use of rules and duties, deliberation and reflection, and even "social contracts" does not emerge from a cruel war of all against all, but rather from a foundation of significant but limited altruism on which rules and reflection build. Huck with affection for Jim is morally good. Huck with principled duty but no affection is an implausible philosophical fantasy, and at best a fast track to moral burnout. Huck with affection *and* principle is ideal. Not affection ruled by principle, nor reason the slave of passion, but sympathetic affection extended and strengthened through rational reflection and rule-following.[9]

# 11

## The Moral Foundations

Morality does not require (though it may be enhanced by) higher reason; and many animals—including humans—live moral lives. But serious questions and challenges remain. The focus has been on what morality is *not*: not the exclusive property of humans, not dependent on reason, and not requiring the accompaniment of moral responsibility. But what are the positive Darwinian implications for morality?

If the question concerns what moral facts or truths are implied by Darwinism, the answer is brief: None. "Darwinian ethics" conjures up the ghosts of social Darwinism: crude principles of "might makes right" driving a war for survival with no quarter given. Social Darwinism was wrong, first, because it ignored the importance of social cooperation and the development of altruism in the evolutionary process. But even more basically, social Darwinism was wrong because Darwinism does not imply any moral facts or objective moral truths, whether social Darwinist or altruistic or otherwise. To the contrary, Darwinism undermines claims for objective morality: our basic moral inclinations or "intuitions" can be explained as species-specific biologically rooted dispositions; they do not require belief in objective, universalizable, cross-species moral truths.

### Ethics without Transcendence

Darwinism undermines *objective* morality, and thus undercuts claims of human moral monopoly that are based on uniquely human powers for discovering objective moral facts. But morality has long been the exclusive property of higher human rationality, and some highly rational humans refuse to surrender their unique moral status without a fight. One important counterattack asserts that Darwinism cannot challenge moral objectivity and the human moral monopoly, simply because Darwinism has *no* implications for morality. Darwinism thus has no implications for moral objectivity and no standing to support the applications of other species for membership in the exclusively human moral club.

Thomas Nagel—in response to E. O. Wilson's suggestion that "the time has come for ethics to be removed temporarily from the hands of the philosophers and biologicized" (1975, 562)—argues that biology has *nothing* to teach us about ethics, because ethics (like mathematics) is an autonomous subject[1] with its own rules and standards:

> . . . ethics is a subject. It is pursued by methods that are continually being developed in response to the problems that arise within it. Obviously the creatures who engage in this activity are organisms about whom we can learn a great deal from biology. Moreover their capacity to perform the reflective and critical tasks involved is presumably somehow a function of their organic structure. But it would be as foolish to seek a biological explanation of ethics as it would be to seek such an explanation of the development of physics. (Nagel 1978, 229)

Nagel is partially correct. Rational reflection can push human morality and ethical theorizing beyond the reach of complete biological explanation. As noted in the previous chapter, reflections (including second-order reflections) on rules and duties can extend and enlarge and strengthen human moral systems, building more elaborate moral structures on the basic moral foundation of sympathy and affection. But Nagel goes further. Ethics, Nagel argues:

> . . . is the result of a human capacity to subject innate or conditioned pre-reflective motivational and behavioral patterns to criticism and revision, and to create new forms of conduct. The capacity to do this presumably has some biological foundation. . . . But the history of the exercise of this capacity and its continual reapplication in criticism and revision of its own products is not part of biology. Biology may tell us about perceptual and motivational starting points, but in its present state it has little bearing on the thinking process by which these starting points are transcended. (Nagel 1978, 230)

Thus biology is tangential to ethics. There may have been some early connection, but ethics has long since transcended such mundane influences and forged its own independent realm of deliberative inquiry, neither driven by nor fettered to biology.

This gives ethics a secure place, where thief cannot rob nor moth corrupt nor sociobiologist trouble; but a price is exacted for that security. The attempt to isolate ethics from biology produces an implausible and ineffectual morality. Kant's ethics is the extreme of such isolation, and it pays the most obvious price. Spontaneous acts of affection, generous works of kindness, immediate heroic efforts to save a friend or loved one: all are excluded from the transcendent ethereal world of pure ethical duty in which sympathies and affections are superseded.

It is true that like physics and mathematics, human morality—enhanced by rational reflection—cannot be "biologicized": cannot be reduced to or explained away by biology. Biology nonetheless provides important basic material for our understanding of morality, and not just an explanation of some remote starting point long since transcended by the powers of human reflection. In human (and nonhuman) morality, the biological foundations form basic commitments that have no analogue in math or physics. Our basic affections and reciprocal inclinations are moral building blocks, but they also function as central vital elements of our moral lives.

To approach the same point from a different angle, consider the contrast between *divergent* moral systems and *common* systems of math and physics. It is difficult to imagine another species with a radically different math or physics from our own. Adopting theirs might require a paradigm shift, but it would be a paradigm shift motivated by common metascientific-mathematical goals. In contrast, it is easy to think of competing moral systems that we could not share. H. L. A. Hart (1961, 189ff) claimed that if humans were protected by bony exoskeletons that made it almost impossible for us to harm one another, then our central moral notions of harm and benefit and our strong prohibition against harming and killing would be very different. But we need not speculate about scaly humans, for there are clear examples of animals having very different basic motives from our own. Konrad Lorenz (1952) describes the behavior of caged doves and roe deer: the stronger will slowly slaughter the weaker, without inhibition, since in their natural unrestricted environment the weaker simply escapes and there is no need of the stronger's inhibition. By contrast, the lethally equipped social carnivores (such as wolves) have a strong inhibition against harming or killing a submissive member of their own group.[2]

Closer to home, among the primates the muriquis (woolly spider monkeys) live in tolerant and (approximately) egalitarian harmony, with a maximum of affectionate sharing and a minimum of aggression (Strier 1992). In contrast, rhesus monkeys put great emphasis on hierarchy and the privileges of dominance (de Waal 1996, 126–127). Dominant rhesus monkeys share very little with subordinates while vigorously punishing complaints and are swiftly and severely aggressive against even slight challenges to the position and privilege of the dominant elite. The contrast between hierarchical-elitist and egalitarian moral perspectives is well known to human primates, and it is not surprising that close analogues of the contrast can be found among our primate cousins.

When we compare ourselves to our more distant relatives there are even more dramatic differences. E. O. Wilson contrasts our moral system with that of highly intelligent ants:

> Our societies are based on the mammalian plan: the individual strives for personal reproductive success foremost and that of his immediate kin secondarily; further grudging cooperation represents a compromise struck in order to enjoy the benefits of group membership. A rational ant—let us imagine for a moment that ants and other social insects had succeeded in evolving high intelligence—would find such an arrangement biologically unsound and the very concept of individual freedom intrinsically evil. (1978, 198)

This difference is hardly surprising. Since we share many of our genes with our community and more with our family, willingness to risk one's self for community and family enhances the survival chances of the shared genes; however, any genetic tendency to be completely self-sacrificing for genetically nonidentical others would be unlikely to spread and survive. But among genetically identical ants a tendency to sacrifice oneself to promote the survival and welfare of the community would become entrenched. Thus if intelligent ants were constructing a code to extend and enhance their moral behavior, the resulting rules would be quite different from ours. Kant's imperative that every individual must be treated as an end and never as a means would strike intelligent ants as morally loathsome.

Fanciful as that story may be, the moral is a simple one: biology is fundamentally important to ethics. The biological roots of our ethical systems are not analogous to the biological foundations of our capacities for doing mathematics or physics, and ethical theory cannot transcend those roots and reduce them to ethical irrelevance. Ethical theorizing, like mathematics, involves higher-order reflective and deliberative activities (and social structures and influences) that cannot be plausibly reduced to their biological foundation. But even at the most sublime (or possibly ridiculous) reaches of ethical theorizing, there remain basic biological motives *within* the ethical system that are not merely the conditions for such theorizing.[3] Thus Kant's "purely rational" system of ethics starts from and is built around a principle (treat all persons as ends-in-themselves) that is not itself rationally derived, but is instead a basic biological inclination that the rational ants would find morally egregious.

Biology plays a part in morality that is more basic and pivotal than a mathematics analogy allows. This is not to suggest that ethics (or even actual human morality) can be biologicized. Something would be lost, including the special rule-following moral extension and strengthening that is a uniquely human contribution. And in some instances (for example, in codifications of procedures for protecting the informed consent of patients or the rights of the accused), the rule-following does have special specific influences on behavior. But recognizing the rational enhancement of morality does not imply that morality transcends biology. Ethics cannot be biologicized, but biology contributes a great deal to the basic development and workings of morality and of ethical systems. Humans enhance and expand our morality through complex combinations of rationality and culture, but there remain moral roots and moral acts that do not require rationality.

## Biological Morality and Moral Truth

Morality cannot transcend its biological roots, but that does not imply some social Darwinist derivation of moral truths from biology. Darwinism does not entail or support any moral principles, whether altruistic or egocentric, kind or cruel. Basic to our moral behavior—whether we are humans, rhesus monkeys, or rational ants—are motives that are not "true moral principles" nor "basic moral facts" and certainly not moral absolutes. They are profoundly felt inclinations. This Darwinist account does not "explain them away," but it does explain away any tendency to accord such deep inclinations a special objective status. It is true, of course, that I feel a deep affection for my children, and for the members of my community, and I feel that it is profoundly good to give them aid and comfort and to reciprocate their kindnesses. That is what I value, and that I value it is a fact. But it is something quite different to suppose that in *addition* to my basic valuing of such affections and inclinations, there is the objective goodness or rightness of that valuing. That additional moral fact is not required, and we get a leaner, less cumbersome moral account if we resist the temptation to add such basic "moral facts."

Of course when we attempt to formalize and order a moral system, we may then accord our basic value inclinations the special status of moral "givens" (or foundational moral principles) much as W. D. Ross (1930) starts from a set of duties that are "intuitively known." Such basic starting points enjoy a special status within a systematized ethics, but no special standing as transsystematic objective moral facts. If we are searching for justifications for our basic moral inclinations, we shall search in vain. But the search for such a justification is misguided, for no justification is needed: it is only the wish to establish such basic inclinations as rational principles transcending our animal nature that has made the need for such justification seem pressing.[4]

Not only is moral objectivity not an implication of Darwinism; to the contrary, moral objectivism (like the requirement of moral rationality) is a traditional way of guarding the exclusive human title to morality. If morality is objective, then the discovery of moral truth can be confined to those who possess some special capacity or privilege—rational deliberation, or intuitive powers, or innately inscribed truths, or divine revelation—that only humans enjoy. A thoroughgoing Darwinism challenges such exclusive human claim to morality, and one important element of that challenge is the challenge to moral objectivity.

## Morality without Objectivity

We can be profoundly moral animals without requiring an ultimately objective basis for our moral inclinations and commitments (or for the principles founded on those inclinations). But that claim must withstand serious challenge. Michael Ruse's (1986) version of Darwinian metaethics rejects objective moral truth in favor of deep moral dispositions that we developed in our evolution as social and cooperative animals. Peter Woolcock (1993) offers a vigorous critique of such nonobjective morality, offering arguments both important and instructive.

Woolcock's critique of Ruse's nonobjective Darwinian metaethics is built on a dilemma: Are ethical principles and imperatives objective, genuinely true, and grounded in fact, existing "independently of our sense of feeling obligated" (Woolcock, 424)? Or is our sense of moral obligation based on "irrational desires" that make it "irrational (because false) to regard ourselves as bound not to behave immorally when we can get away with it" (Woolcock 1993, 428)? Either obligations must be rationally based on objectively true moral facts, or moral obligations and principles are mere fantasies with no legitimate claims upon us. As Woolcock states the stark quandary:

> If sentences like "A is under an obligation to do X" are never literally true, then normative theories such as utilitarianism, contractarianism or even Darwinian normative ethics are just fiction and fairy stories. (1993, 429–430)

Those are the possibilities: objective independent truths or fairy tales.

Starting from this dilemma, it is a short step to the vital importance of objectivist ethics. My obligation to care for my children, my visceral revulsion toward torture, my deep moral opposition to elitist exploitation: surely these are more than fiction and foolishness. So they must be objectively true moral principles and obligations.

The problem, of course, is in the initial dilemma premise. If moral claims and obligations are not based on literal factual truth, then the only alternative Woolcock can imagine is fantasy and fraud: the sort of foundation on which no reasonable person would wish to base important decisions. That fundamental false dilemma is clear in the following illustration offered by Woolcock:

> Suppose . . . a woman . . . wants to act only on true beliefs. Such a person has a reason to at least sometimes give the interests of other people equal or superior weighting to her own as long as she believes the sentence "I have at least one moral obligation" to be true. . . . But, once she accepts Ruse's arguments, she will realise that her sense of obligation is totally misleading. All that she will be left with as conscious reasons for actions will be her own wants, inclinations, preferences, feelings etc. which may or may not coincide with what morality requires. In particular, she will be left with no reason to act contrary to her own wishes when she wants to do something that harms the interests of others and she can successfully avoid detection and punishment. . . . (1993, 424)

All of that is true, given the assumption from which Wool-cock starts: someone who "wants to act only on true beliefs." That sounds innocent enough: it's certainly better than acting on false beliefs. However, this seemingly innocent assumption sets in place the false dichotomy that is at the heart of Woolcock's argument. Either we are acting on true, rationally justified beliefs, or we are acting arbitrarily and without enduring conviction. Either we are acting on true beliefs, or we are left with "only feelings" that have no substance and no staying power.

But there are other alternatives.On a Darwinian naturalist view, there is ultimately no rational justification for our basic moral dispositions: ultimately we are not acting on true beliefs but instead on deeply rooted evolved motives. As Ruse states:

> Thanks to evolution, humans have innate dispositions to believe that we should promote the general happiness, and that we should treat people as ends rather than means. (1986, 251)

But such dispositions are not a source of objective moral truth. To the contrary, ethical principles are:

> . . . subjective, being a function of human nature, and reducing ultimately to feelings and sentiments—feelings and sentiments of a type different from wishes and desires, but ultimately emotions of some kind. . . . (1986, 252)

Our moral obligations are not based on true moral facts or objective obligations, but on the fundamental dispositions that our species evolved. Ruse makes the point quite graphically:

We are what we are because we are recently evolved from savannah-dwelling primates. Suppose that we had evolved from cave-dwellers, or some such thing. We might have as our highest principle of moral obligation the imperative to eat each others' faeces. Not simply the desire, but the obligation. (1986, 263)

Whatever the plausibility of such an alternative cave-dweller ethic, Ruse's point is plain: the roots of our moral inclinations are shaped by our evolutionary history and require no ultimate underpinning from Reason or God or objective moral truths. But that does not place such basic moral principles under the rubric of fabulous fairy stories and irrational delusions, nor into the category of "mere feelings" or whimsy. They are our deepest commitments, our heartfelt principles, our fundamental values. They are not rational, nor derived from rational reflection; but neither are they irrational, nor is it irrational to cherish and champion them. They are not merely rules we follow (as one might grudgingly observe a speed limit) only because some authority is watching and we cannot get away with violations. Absence of rational justification does not undermine our commitment to our moral obligations, just as, analogously, our love and commitment to our spouses and children may remain steadfast without either rational grounding or external sanction.

So Ruse's Darwinian account rejects both the existence of and the need for objective morality. Objective morality dies hard, however; and Ruse himself—having developed a clear and effective account of the Darwinian nonobjective roots of basic ethical dispositions and "intuitions"—cannot resist ascribing a central role to *belief* in moral objectivity. Ruse's suggestion that morality requires the illusion of objectivity shows the strength and pervasiveness of the temptation to intellectualize moral principles. It is most evident in Kant, but even a thoroughly Darwinian empiricist like Ruse is not immune to its charms, positing a vital role for *belief* in the cognitive objectivity of moral principles even as he undercuts any genuine rational foundation.

Ruse claims that morality requires an illusion of moral objectivity because:

. . . the big weakness of traditional subjectivism is that it fails to account for the true nature of our moral experience. The

> whole point about morality is that it is binding, not open to
> individual choice. It is greater than and above any of us.
> (1986, 252)

But while other forms of subjectivism or noncognitivism may
run aground here, Ruse insists that "Darwinism can handle
this point." And Darwinism handles it thus:

> The Darwinian argues that morality simply does not work
> (from a biological perspective), unless we believe that it is
> objective. Darwinian theory shows that, in fact, morality is a
> function of (subjective) feelings; but it shows also that we have
> (and must have) the illusion of objectivity. (1986, 253)

The objectivity illusion is required (according to Ruse) in order
for this moral adaptation "to get us to go beyond regular wishes,
desires and fears, and to interact socially with people." (1986,
253) The moral adaptation accomplishes this:

> by filling us full of thoughts about obligations and duties, and
> so forth. And the key to what is going on is that we are then
> moved to action, precisely because we think morality is some-
> thing laid upon us. . . . If morality did not have this air of exter-
> nality or objectivity, it would not be morality and (from a bio-
> logical perspective) would fail to do what it is intended to do.
> (1986, 253)

But just here Ruse turns his very plausible Darwinian
account of ethics upside down. His account explains, and quite
cogently, why we should be tempted to ascribe objectivity to our
most basic value motives. But nothing in that account shows
that such an "illusion of objectivity" is essential to the functioning of morality. Indeed, Ruse himself gives excellent reasons
for believing such an illusion is not required: the testimony of
his own experience, and the experience of many others who
have rejected belief in the fundamental objectivity of moral
obligations. As Ruse puts it:

> In the case of morality, we are all part of the game, and even
> those of us who realize this [who realize that ethics is nonob-
> jective] have no desire to drop out. (1986, 257)

But if those who reject the objectivity of ethics can and do continue to believe in and follow their moral obligations and values,

then the "illusion of objectivity" is not necessary for morality to function.

Furthermore, Ruse offers—in the very chapter in which he asserts the need for an illusion of objectivity—compelling evidence against any such requirement. He cites examples of moral behavior among chimpanzees, noting that in observations of a band of semi-wild chimpanzees at Arnhem Zoo:

> Time and again, the primatologists have seen behaviour which differs not at all from human moral behaviour. (1986, 228)

On the basis of those examples, it is quite plausible to suppose that chimpanzees act morally, including such moral acts as intragroup peacemaking. But it is highly implausible (and excessively complicated) to suggest that the moral chimp peacemakers are motivated by an illusion of objectivity. It is one thing to suppose that chimps act morally, from deep-rooted moral dispositions that can overcome immediate desires. It is something else again to suppose that they believe their moral behavior to be directed by objective moral truths.

So there are powerful counterexamples to Ruse's claim that morality requires an illusion of objectivity. Chimpanzees and rhesus monkeys (Rachels 1990, 147–152) and perhaps many other animals act morally, and presumably without convictions—or illusions—concerning moral objectivity. And surely one could find at least some instances of moral behavior in the lives of David Hume, Charles Darwin, A. J. Ayer, Rudolf Carnap, Herbert Feigl, J. L. Mackie, B. F. Skinner, Bernard Williams, and Michael Ruse, all of whom have managed without the illusion of moral objectivity.[5]

Still, the belief that ethics requires objectivity illusions is a persistent one. Bernard Williams believes that ethics rests on certain deep dispositions but that we can never completely acknowledge that foundation:

> I have tried to say why ethical thought has no chance of being everything it seems. Even if ethical thought had a foundation in determinate conceptions of well-being [which Williams thinks unlikely], the consequences of that could lie only in justifying a *disposition to accept* certain ethical statements, rather than in showing, directly, the truth of those statements: but this is not how it would naturally appear to those who accepted them. (Williams 1985, 199)

The upshot of this, according to Williams, is that "ethical thought will never entirely appear as what it is, and can never fully manifest the fact that it rests in human dispositions. . . ." (Williams 1985, 199–200); except, that is, to philosophers and biologists, who continue to take ethics seriously while recognizing its foundation in dispositions rather than objective moral fact. Apparently the illusion of ethical objectivity is required, but only for the vulgar.

But in fact the vulgar may have less need of ethical objectivity than do the philosophers. That we should have deep and steadfast commitments—to family, friends, and community, as well as to schools and football teams—that do not rely on reason and objectivity is neither surprising nor disturbing, and that our basic moral commitments might fall into that category (on a par with our commitment to family and friends) is problematic only if one supposes that there must be a foundation in reason for all our deepest motivations. If we enlarge our moral outlook to include the moral behavior of other species, it will be even less likely to upset or surprise us when we recognize that basic moral dispositions are not grounded in either objectivity or rationality.

We do not require an illusion of objectivity in order to live a good and steadfast moral life. But there is an important grain of truth in Ruse's insistence on an illusion of moral objectivity. Bernard Williams notes that our basic ethical convictions are not matters of *choice*. As Williams states:

> You could not have an ethical conviction, and be conscious that it was the product of a decision, unless that decision itself appeared inescapable. (Williams 1985, 169)

The claim that we *never* choose our ethical convictions may be too strong; but in any case, typically we do not. Our ethical convictions are our deepest commitments, stemming from our biological and social histories. They may be rejected or modified, but we do not generally *choose* them any more than we choose to love our children. That does not mean we must believe they are objective truths; but neither does it mean that they are lightly held beliefs that we are ready to discard, much less that they are felt as alien impositions from which we long to escape.

Of course if one has invested heavily in divine commandments or the stern dictates of pure Reason or a transcendent realm of moral truth, then any morality based on nonrational animal affections and dispositions and commitments may suffer by invidious comparison. For example, Woolcock regards the following as almost a *reductio* of Ruse's Darwinian metaethics:

> Ruse, however, will not allow obligations to be mind-independent in the sense that each of us has an obligation not to enslave people, regardless of whether any of us ever has such a sense of obligation. (1993, 424)

And that is true: Ruse's Darwinian metaethics cannot find room for moral principles or obligations existing in splendid objective isolation from any dispositions or commitments. But unless one requires that morality have the sanction of God or some secular substitute, that is not distressing. After all, many of us profoundly and viscerally detest the egregious *moral* wrong of slavery. That commitment requires no imprimatur from Reason or deity or objectivity to enhance its deep moral status. This nonobjective morality—not imposed by any objective or divine or outside authority—is firmly fixed by our own deepest dispositions and commitments.

Thus to deny the objectivity of moral principles and obligations is not to regard them as irrational. Woolcock points out that a woman who (learning from Ruse) now regards moral beliefs as nonobjective would have "no true beliefs sufficient to stop her from stealing or murdering if she so wished" (425). But while she might have no "true beliefs" to counteract her occasional homicidal or larcenous wishes, she may still have profound moral commitments and attachments that would oppose such desires. And these commitments are her own: not rationally based, but not irrational accretions that she longs to escape. To suppose that all our nonrational commitments must be felt as irrational alien burdens is to vastly overintellectualize our nature and to ignore obvious counterexamples: our nonrational (but not irrational and not alien) moral commitments to our families and friends, and our nonmoral—and certainly nonrational—dedication to favorite teams and towns and taverns.

Ruse's simpler Darwinian account places a heavy burden of proof on the moral objectivist. Obviously Ruse does not show that there is no objective basis for morality; however, he does show that we can explain moral behavior—and profound moral commitments that push well beyond immediate desires—more

economically by tracing the causes to deep biological dispositions. As noted, Ruse adds the unnecessary "illusion of moral
objectivity" complication; but that can be excised without compromising the genuine accomplishment of Ruse's general Darwinian account of morality. Morality requires neither the substance nor the illusion of objectivity.

Woolcock, however, argues that Ruse's moral objectivity
illusion cannot be so easily discarded. Woolcock claims that if
people who could get away with violating moral rules and obligations continued to act morally *without* belief in moral objectivity, then "this would strongly suggest an irresistible genetic tendency" toward moral behavior, and Woolcock finds decisive
empirical evidence against such an iresistible tendency:

> As it happens, there are only far too many people willing to
> break the social rules when they can get away with it, so there
> seems to be no case for this kind of genetic tendency either.
> (1993, 427)

Woolcock is correct that there is little evidence in humans
for an "irresistible genetic tendency" toward moral behavior. But
Darwinism does not suggest such a human (or chimpanzee)
"irresistible genetic tendency." It is not even clear what would
count: after all, an "irresistible" tendency would be transformed
from tendency to tropism. If instead there is, as Ruse suggests,
a strong (not irresistible) genetic *tendency* toward moral behavior, then we would expect—as indeed we find—that some individuals are more oriented toward that tendency, and that the
tendency can be enhanced or inhibited by varying environments (such a genetic tendency may find more fertile ground
among a well-functioning Quaker community than in a starving
and desperate group of Ik tribesmen). The tendency may be
strengthened or weakened, activated or atrophied, by the right
(or wrong) training, opportunity, environment. So Ruse's causal
analysis is supported by (is at the very least compatible with)
the available evidence, and provides a lean but effective naturalistic nonobjectivist Darwinian metaethics.

In sum, the Darwinian critique of moral objectivity can
withstand counterarguments. The supposed objectivity of
morality is an illusion, as Ruse argues. But though the illusion
may have had some uses and even some limited benefits, it is
so far from being essential to the functioning of morality that it

is more likely to be an impediment. Rather than worrying about—to use Woolcock's comfortable metaphor—"letting the cat out of the bag" by revealing the nonobjectivity of morality, we should welcome the release of this particular feline into harsh light and hard scrutiny. The illusion of moral objectivity is not doing the essential work, and the illusion has kept us from looking carefully and empirically at the basic motivations that fuel morality, how they can be strengthened and fostered, and in what environments they flourish. So long as the illusion of objectivity distorts our view and limits such investigation, failure of emotive moral commitments will continue to be condemned and blamed, but seldom understood. And so long as discovery of "objective moral truths" requires special human powers (of rationality or intuition or demi-divinity), "true morality" will remain exclusively human and examination of morality within a larger biological context will be ruled out of order.

The conclusion is that moral behavior of humans (and other animals) can flourish without moral objectivity (and without the illusion of moral objectivity). That conclusion must still withstand further challenges—in fact, so many challenges that one could hardly list them, much less answer them. But examining some of the most significant challenges will make clearer the key features of the Darwinian metaethics that extends a *non*objective morality *beyond* humans.

# 12

---

## Darwinian Moral Nonobjectivism

Morality does not require a foundation of objective moral truth, and a simpler clearer view of morality—a view that is more compatible with Darwinian biology—emerges when the search for basic moral truths is abandoned. That is not to suggest that biology proves the truth of moral nonobjectivism. Rather, moral nonobjectivism is a better *fit* with Darwinism, and with scientific naturalism in general. But that claim is hotly disputed by contemporary advocates of moral objectivism who call themselves "moral realists." Moral realists insist that there are natural moral facts: objective moral truths that can be discovered and confirmed in the natural world, without appeal to mysterious moral intuitions or God's will or transcendent forms or principles of pure Reason. And moral realists maintain that science is on the moral objectivist side—or at least that scientific naturalism is more compatible with moral *objectivism* than with moral nonobjectivism.

### Moral Realism vs. Darwinian Nonobjectivism

An interesting version of that moral realist argument is developed by Woolcock. As the final thrust of his attack on Ruse's version of nonobjectivist Darwinian metaethics, Woolcock criticizes Ruse's analysis of the *causal* (as opposed to objective justificatory *reasons*) foundations of morality. Woolcock claims that the same reasons/causes distinction that Ruse finds in ethics also applies to science, and since the reasons/causes distinction in science does not undermine scientific objectivity, the analogous distinction in morality does not

143

threaten moral objectivity. This is an interesting argument, and examining it yields a clearer picture of Darwinian *non*objectivist metaethics.

Woolcock begins with Ruse's acknowledgment that the criteria for good science—simplicity, causal regularity, consilience, falsifiability—are a matter of general agreement among scientists. Thus when a scientist has given such reasons for preferring one theory to another, then (as Woolcock states):

> There are no further reasons a scientist can offer to justify his or her choice of theory in so far as the goal of his choice is to arrive at the theory most likely to be true. After all, what counts as justifying his or her choice seems to be nothing more than showing that it meets the criteria of rational theory choice. So, if we are to go further, if we need an explanation of why scientists want their theories to conform to the criteria of rational theory choice, then we will have to step outside of the justification game, that is, the game that concerns itself with which theories are true, into the causal game. (1993, 433–434)

When we reach that point, we must ask why scientists prefer such theories—and ultimately we shall find causes, rather than justifications. Woolcock draws the moral of the story:

> So, if the reasons/causes distinction breaks down in the moral case, then it also breaks down in exactly the same way in the scientific case. Ultimate justification in morals is no worse off than ultimate justification in science. Both forms of justification come to an end and, when they do, any further explanation will be causal rather than justificatory. (1993, 434)

And if reaching such a justificatory limit does not threaten the objectivity of science, then an analogous limit poses no threat to moral objectivity.

The fact that science presupposes values has been a source of great interest and profound comfort to moral realists. Peter Railton develops a similar argument against A. J. Ayer's assault on moral objectivism. Railton attacks Ayer's claim that "argument is possible on moral questions only if some system of values is presupposed" (Ayer 1952, 111). He argues that that is grounds for ethical nonobjectivism only if one is prepared to accept scientific nonobjectivism as well. For as Railton notes:

What it would be rational for an individual to believe on the basis of a given experience will vary not only with respect to his other beliefs, but also with respect to what he desires. From this it follows that no amount of mere argumentation or experience could force one on pain of irrationality to accept even the factual claims of empirical science. . . . Unfortunately for the contrast Ayer wished to make, we find that argument is possible on scientific questions only if some system of values is presupposed. (Railton 1986, 167)

Along similar lines Geoffrey Sayre-McCord (1988, 277) notes the essential role of evaluations and evaluative facts in science and then argues that since in science the notion of "best explanations" involves values and value judgments, those who accept the essential role of value judgments in factual scientific investigations should not deny that values and moral facts can play an equally legitimate role in moral explanations.[1]

Science does presuppose values, as the moral realists insightfully note; but the nonobjectivist contrast between science and ethics remains, and it remains important. The science/ethics contrast is not between inquiries and debates and explanations in ethics that presuppose values, and scientific inquiries-debates-explanations that do not: in short, not an invidious contrast between the objectivity of science and the subjectivity of ethics. For Railton is right that "argument is possible on scientific questions only if some system of values is presupposed." After all, scientific argument is daily rendered impossible by fundamental differences in values. If, for example, we consider blasphemous any efforts to understand and control God's miraculous creation, valuing instead a childlike uncritical faith, then scientific arguments are unlikely to gain much purchase on our thinking. Scientific investigation does presuppose basic values, such as commitment to maximizing precise prediction and control of phenomena. Thus science and ethics are on equal footing in requiring value presuppositions.

Still, the analogy offered by Woolcock and Railton and Sayre-McCord is not accurate. Science does reach a justificatory limit, just as ethics does. But when science reaches its limit and turns its spade, justification resources are not yet exhausted: one may turn to justification by appeal to basic shared values (a justification within a shared framework of *ethical*—rather than scientific—principles). For example, a scientist may acknowledge the general principles of science, but still ask: "Is the pursuit of science really (morally) good?" Here the scientist has moved out of science, and the question posed is ethical. It may (or may not) be resolved for the questioner at that ethical level: "Yes, pursuit of science is good, because pursuit of truth is the proper and highest good for humanity" or "Science is good because science helps relieve suffering and it is morally good to relieve suffering." But suppose such ethical justifications are challenged, and the resulting ethical questions are pursued to their rational justificatory far limits: as, for example, when one places the greatest value on the pursuit of new discoveries and another champions static secure orthodoxy, or one thinks all suffering an evil to be eliminated and another values suffering as a vital element of the richness of life. In that case there is no further justificatory domain available, and the remaining intractable disputes are enduringly ethical. Such unresolved disputes undercut the objectivity of ethics in a way that is not analogous to the queries that arise *within* the given framework of scientific principles.

Given the goals of science, we cannot contrive other principles or practices that would yield them. Whether one's origins are caves or savannahs, earthly or extraterrestrial, if one shares the basic goals of science, then we know of no alternative values for effectively pursuing those goals. So lack of ultimate justification need not disturb the scientist. As scientist, she can answer challenges to her scientific principles in terms of their unique effectiveness for achieving the shared and generally definitive goals and values (prediction, discovery, control) of the scientific enterprise. The exact dimensions of those values may be vague, and certainly one can reject scientific values such as prediction and control (religious fanatics and ideologues often do so); but one cannot reject the basic defining values of the scientific enterprise and continue to be a scientist. One can pretend to be doing science (but instead be perpetrating a fraudulent pseudoscience, such as creationism); or one can argue that some alternative system (with values other than those of science) is better than science (as Pascal, for example, became convinced when he renounced scientific research in favor of faith). But one does scientific work only by adhering to basic scientific values. Obviously there are some fuzzy areas and vexed questions when we attempt to trace the values definitive of science, and especially so in any attempt to rank those values. Nonetheless, there are some basic accepted values governing and defining scientific inquiry. If one has no interest in pre-diction, refuses to allow for the possibility that one's theories might be disconfirmed, steadfastly prefers theories that offer less rather than more control of the phenomena, and rejects all use of observation, then one has stepped beyond the bound-aries of science, even if it is difficult to say precisely where those boundaries lie.

This appeal to definitive scientific values may seem an atavistic throwback to logical positivism, out of step with a holistic-pragmatic age in which all "scientific facts" are subject to revision and the most cherished scientific principles can be rejected. But even in that context, there remain definitive sci-entific values that cannot be rejected without rejecting science. A scientist may decide that in this case the value of making pre-cise predictions carries less weight than the value of an ele-gantly unified theory; but rather than rejecting the value of pre-dictive power, the scientist is compromising it in favor of another scientific value. That the predictive value has not been rejected becomes obvious when the elegant theory grievously violates that predictive value, and is thus rejected, or when a new theory with both theoretical elegance and maximum pre-dictive power is happily adopted. Thus there remain definitive scientific values that scientists continue to hold even when the values are compromised.

If those basic scientific goals and values are challenged ("comfortable religious orthodoxy is more morally worthy than the arrogant search for potentially disturbing discoveries"), then the issue must be passed over into ethics. Such a challenge questions the proper place and worth of objective scientific inquiry within our framework of basic moral values, but it is not a challenge to scientific objectivity.

The situation is quite different when we reach basic ethi-cal and evaluative inquiries. At that level we cannot turn the value questions over to some other domain. Although we may justify some of our values in terms of others ("I value equal edu-cational opportunity because of my egalitarian principles"), eventually we reach the point at which no more basic value principles are available for appeal. Then we do not (as in sci-ence) have the luxury of assuming shared basic goals: at that level the basic goals are precisely what are being queried, and there is the possibility of intractable fundamental disagreement over those goals and values. As noted in the previous chapter, if ants evolved higher intelligence while retaining the same reproductive processes and genetic links, they likely would regard our emphasis on individual rights—and the insistence that no individual be treated as a means—as not merely absurd, but morally odious. But such fanciful examples are not required. We are only too aware that within our own species there is the possibility—and the actuality—of fundamentally different and categorically opposed basic moral principles (as between egalitarian and elitist-aristocratic value systems). When disputing such views, we may eventually find that there is no shared set of values on which to base arguments. Thus reason and argument may end without any rational means of resolving the conflict, and no basic value framework can be assumed without begging the question against alternatives that (however repugnant we may find them) are genuine and coherent. In such cases we can seek the causes of such differing moral dispositions, but we are at the end of justification.[2]

Of course one may insist that science itself ultimately rests on value premises that are nonobjective. But that only means that scientific principles are favored by scientists because they are the best means of accomplishing what scientists *value*: namely, scientific knowledge and the possibility of prediction and control. If you don't value that, then don't do science: be an artist, or a priest, or a poet, or a prophet—or a philosopher, for that matter. Let a hundred flowers bloom, and if you don't like the blossoms of science, then pick some other bouquet. But with basic *ethical* premises, things are not so easy. I cannot be comfortable with your elitist values if I favor egalitarian principles. I can do science while you do religion, but I cannot do egalitarianism while you construct an elitist society all around me. And if your religious ethics promotes intolerance of free scientific inquiry, then our clash of basic values will not be easily resolved; if the conflict reaches down to our basic values, it cannot be resolved at all by rational means.

### Megaethical Nonobjectivism

Moral realists, however, sometimes claim that there *are* basic definitive values for the ethical enterprise, just as there are for science. Ethics is concerned with general human flourishing, and human flourishing involves satisfaction of human needs and goods. Thus Boyd, in giving lessons on "How to Be a Moral Realist," notes that "there are a number of important human goods, things that satisfy important human needs," such as needs for love, friendship, and artistic expression. He then states that:

> Moral goodness is defined by this cluster of goods and the homeostatic mechanisms which unify them. Actions, policies, character traits, etc. are morally good to the extent to which they tend to foster the realization of these goods or to develop and sustain the homeostatic mechanisms upon which their unity depends. (Boyd 1988, 203)

Along similar lines, Railton claims that "moral norms reflect a certain kind of rationality, rationality not from the point of view of any particular individual, but from what might be called a social point of view." And such social rationality seeks "what would be rationally approved of were the interests of all potentially affected individuals counted equally under circumstances of full and vivid information." (Railton 1986, 190) Railton notes that this will not give us absolute, cosmic moral facts; but it does yield "a form of moral realism that is essentially tied to a limited point of view, an impartial yet human one." (Railton 1986, 200) Thus Railton claims that his moral realism:

> gives us a way of understanding how moral values or imperatives might be objective without being cosmic. They need be grounded in nothing more transcendental than facts about man and his environment, facts about what sorts of things matter to us, and how the ways we live affect these things. (Railton 1986, 201)

As in science, the exact range of the ethics-defining values may be fuzzy, but nonetheless there are such ethics-defining values, and those who reject them are not participating in the ethical enterprise. It is possible to reject those values (one may be an amoralist, or an irrational egoist, or a moral monster); but the ethical enterprise endures, and to be part of that ethical community requires agreement with the basic ethics-defining principles. Of course there remains space *within* ethics for disagreement, but—just as in science—ethical disagreements can be rationally debated and (in principle) rationally resolved.

From there the moral of moral realism follows easily.

Ethics is analogous to science: both have basic definitive principles, and both have room for rational debate and research and discovery within their respective systems. Science is the paradigmatic realm of facts, and ethics (moral realists claim) has an exactly equal realist claim to debating and discovering and establishing real moral facts.

Certainly moral realists are correct that within a given ethical system (defined by basic shared value assumptions) moral realism reigns supreme: there are natural investigations to be made, facts to be discovered, disagreements to be rationally deliberated. At that level, there is ethical realism-objectivism the equal of scientific objectivism. But ethical *non*objectivism does not deny that, *given* a presupposed value framework (whether in science or in ethics), objective arguments and investigations and discoveries are possible. Instead, ethical nonobjectivism insists that when *fundamental* value conflicts arise and basic value questions are posed, then the disputes and values are not objective. And such conflict and challenge is possible in ethics in a manner that is not possible in science.

Science does presuppose basic values, as already noted. But challenges to the basic values of science become questions of ethics. "Should we pursue science?" That is an ethical rather than a scientific question. In contrast, the question whether we should follow the basic values of an ethical system (such as the values elegantly described by Boyd, or some radically different ethical system) *remains* an ethical question. Thus—in contrast to science—ethics cannot be confined to intraethics: there are inevitably interethical issues as well. Or to put it another way, nonobjectivist metaethics acknowledges that there are moral facts within given ethical systems, or intraethically; but nonobjectivists also note the possibility of *inter*ethical disputes that arise concerning competing value systems. In those deep disputes, the basic value frameworks are challenged and thus the frameworks cannot be assumed without question-begging. It is at that level that nonobjectivism applies: the level of "megaethics" (we might call it) at which the most fundamental ethical-framework-defining questions are posed.

Consider the claim that: if you reject the value of the general flourishing of all human beings, then you have no concern for ethics, and you are not raising a meaningful ethical question. That is transparently a *mega*ethical tactic. It is a persuasive definition that attempts to emotively influence those who disagree, rather than a rational argument. For certainly it is possible to consistently propose and follow an ethical system—such as elitism—that disputes the general-concern ethical system. If one upbraids the elitist (who is unconcerned with the welfare of most humans) for "not really doing ethics," the answers are too easy. The elitist does not care what it is called: elitism is a consistent value system that is not subject to rational refutation by "ethical" opponents. (Of course the elitist system does not promote *general* human flourishing; but in a dispute with the elitist, such a value cannot be assumed without begging the question). Thus the question can and does arise of whether to follow a general flourishing value-ethical system. And that meaningful and challenging question cannot—as in science—be dismissed as a question belonging to another realm. Scientists easily dismiss those who reject prediction and control as scientific values: scientists read them out of the scientific enterprise, as people who have different interests and values and do not wish to pursue science. But there is no analogous dismissal for those who favor radically different ethical systems, for ethics must include the megaethical realm of basic system-defining values. Science shifts its megaquestions to ethics, but ethics—at the megaethical level—must face them.

Genuine "megaethical" questions can and do challenge the moral realists' general-human-flourishing value system. First, why should there be concern with *all* humans (rather than a much narrower special elite, with the elite being defined in terms of whatever intellectual or esthetic or power norms one chooses). And questions also arise from the other direction: should concern be exclusively for all *humans*?[3] Does that include the severely defective, comparable in intellectual ability to dogs or pigs? Should we draw the line at groundhogs? mosquitoes? viruses? Should the concern extend even to the inanimate realm? Perhaps there should be greater concern for the inanimate than for humans: Robinson Jeffers values storms, cliffs, and oceans, asserting in one poem that "their beauty has more meaning than the whole human race." One can, quite consistently, consider it not very important that the human species survive. Indeed, according to some megaethical views the world would be a better place in the absence of our species. Short of that, it is possible to question whether maximizing human flourishing is the defining purpose of ethics: the question of whether humans should instead regard themselves as only one small part of a more significant universe, and concern themselves with some transhuman goal, is a genuine moral question. Such radical alternative value systems are not refutable by appeal to any given moral facts or basic values, for the realm of ethics (megaethics) is precisely where such basic values are proposed and challenged, favored and rejected.

In short, we can rule out of order certain questions about the realism of science, but not the analogous ethical questions. So long as moral realism is confined to intrasystematic considerations, moral realism is as legitimate as scientific realism. But there are within ethics—unlike within science—legitimate megaquestions, that are (notwithstanding the cognitive moral realism that guides intraethics) nonobjective. Morality is systematically real, but ultimately ideal.

The naturalist moral realist may resist this conclusion by pointing out natural tendencies in our species, our basic human goals-intents-desires. For example, both Boyd (1988, 209) and Lycan (1986, 89) note that our evolutionary history may well account for our capacities to reliably recognize the fundamental needs of ourselves and of others and may also account for the existence of our non-self-interested desires. And such capacities and desires have a special degree of trustworthiness (Boyd and Lycan argue), since they have evolved as mechanisms that enhance our collective survival and welfare.

It is not surprising to find altruistic, cooperative, nonself-interested inclinations in humans. Such inclinations facilitate the cooperative behavior that has enabled our species—short in tooth, soft in skin, and slow afoot—to survive and prosper. I am not denying, and certainly not disparaging, such affectionate cooperative tendencies: from my own value perspective, they are the best aspect of human behavior and the best hope of a decent human future. Such "intuitive" feelings or desires may be useful in promoting general human well-being and "our collective survival and welfare," and thus may be excellent guides to moral facts within the "general-human-flourishing" ethical framework. Still, they do not establish objective *mega*ethical facts. For it is quite possible to acknowledge such human capacities and tendencies and still deny that those are the correct values. One might consider our "natural" tendency to altruistic cooperation a weakness or flaw in our species and instead value our tendencies toward aggression.[4] Altruistic tendencies are the most promising path to cooperative human behavior and the general flourishing of all members of our species, but that does not exempt cooperative flourishing values from megaethical challenge.

Moral realists, such as Lowell Kleiman, accurately note that "cultures that are opposed to genocide, and killing in general, are more likely to be at peace with their neighbors." And that leads, by way of a rhetorical question, to moral facts: "Peace among nations is a moral goal. Why is it difficult to see any moral facts behind the achievement of a moral goal?" (Kleiman 1989, 166) The answer is that it is not difficult to see moral facts behind the achievement of that goal, but such moral facts can be seen only *within* a system of presupposed basic moral principles. If those moral principles are called into question, then the "moral facts" cannot be employed to hold the system in place. Such "moral facts" exist within the given system, but they cannot be used to establish objectivist *mega*ethics. For at the megaethical level there are alternatives, even to our cherished value of peaceful altruistic cooperation. One of Ezra Pound's poems describes such an alternative, celebrating "the battle's rejoicing" and pronouncing this curse: "May God damn for ever all who cry 'Peace!'" And Pound's poetic voice is but an echo of King David's, who sings verses of praise (Ps. 18) to the "God that girdeth me with strength" and "teacheth my hands to war."

While we may (given our own basic values) find such sentiments appalling, it is quite clear that such "intuitions" also form a part of human society. As much as we may oppose and condemn them, it is something else to suppose that we can establish as moral fact the superiority of the peaceable, cooperative framework. Such megaethical proofs are impossible because the basic standards by which proof would be judged are here called into question. Of course we may easily show that the warlike ways Pound celebrates are profoundly harmful to human welfare, and that they inflict enormous suffering on huge numbers of human beings, and that—in an age of thermonuclear swords—they may lead to human extinction. But subscribers to such a martial ethic might well acknowledge that their moral system makes life nasty, brutish, and short, and nonetheless place great value on such a system, even maintaining that the thrill of a brutal warlike life is enhanced by its uncertainty and brevity. If there are shared values, then one may give cogent arguments against celebrating war. Within the system that values general human flourishing, the virtue of altruistic peaceful reconciliatory behavior is a natural moral fact. But when basic systemic conflicts occur—and we are opposed, at the megaethical level, by someone who does not share our basic value system—then there is no recourse to such moral "facts": the moral facts are internally real, but megaethically unreal.

To see the nonobjectivism that dominates the megaethical level (and the futility of appeals to "moral facts" at that megaethical nonobjective level), suppose it were discovered that our species requires enormous doses of brutality and elitist exploitation for our long-term flourishing, and that cooperation and altruism would sap the vitality of the species and ultimately reduce its prospects for survival. That would not establish the truth of—the megaethical moral fact of—the rightness of brutality and exploitation. Instead, we might well conclude that a briefer span of cooperative and egalitarian survival is preferable to enduringly successful savagery. Therefore in the actual case in which our "flourishing" is enhanced by a more cooperative and peaceful system, that fact does not establish the overall truth of a cooperative system of ethics. For if the facts were quite different, our cooperative ethical system would not be undermined; and if a supposed underpinning can be pulled away while the system remains firmly in place, we are justified in concluding that something else must be holding the system secure. That something else—at the megaethical level—is nonobjective.

Certainly we can reason about morality: for well or ill, this chapter has done precisely that. But at the roots of our morality—whether humans or chimps or white-footed mice—lie basic megaethical moral inclinations that are nonobjective and that do not require (nor even permit) rational support. Since acts motivated by these basic moral motives remain moral, reason is not required for moral acts, and animals other than and in addition to rational humans can be and are moral animals. Morality, then, has its roots in animal affections rather than human reason. The implications of that nonrational animal moral rootedness is the subject of the concluding chapter.

# 13

---

## Conclusion:
## Darwinist Care Ethics

No scientific information—biological or otherwise—can establish basic moral truths. Rather than excluding biology from morality, that opens a fundamental role for biology in the understanding of morality. Morality is founded on our most basic sympathies and affections, developed from our social learning history and, ultimately, our genetically-shaped inclinations. Our basic values and deepest cares are subject to modification, enhancement, extension, and codification through human intellectual capacities; but the rational processes operate from and build upon the materials supplied by our affections.

Recognizing human moral systems as enhancements of animal nonrational morality resolves some vexing tensions in moral philosophy. The capacity to act from duty—even in the absence of sympathy or affection—is a remarkable capacity. It moves morality beyond immediate personal attachments and holds moral behavior on a steadier course than could be charted solely by our emotions and affections. But for all its majesty, we (Kant excepted) may regard duty with ambivalence. If a friend must be prodded by duty to offer a present, the gift has little appeal. If I care for my children from obligation rather than love, the effects may be more detrimental than beneficial. And the greater my suspicion that your hospital call was motivated by duty instead of affectionate concern, the less cheer I take from your visit.[1] The duty-affection split is deep, and reconciliation seems difficult. Emphasizing one at the expense of the other leaves a gap in morality; trying to have both creates a tension.

The tension dissolves when duty-based moral systems are viewed as enhancements of animal morality. Duty keeps indirect reciprocity in place during periods when affection weakens and can broaden and strengthen our commitment to indirect reciprocity beyond the limits of personal relations and affections. But precisely those features that make duty effective in moral enhancement limit its use with friends and family. Michael Stocker (1976) rightly notes that using the principles of duty in our relations with family and friends is destructive, but that does not reveal a schizophrenic split in our morality. Rather than a tension between two opposed parts of morality, the morality of affection and the morality of duty serve different but complementary functions. Rule-following morality can sustain and extend moral behavior, but it cannot supplant the fundamental moral acts stemming from care and affection.

## Care Ethics and Beyond

That explains why the feminist emphasis on the sorely neglected care and trust and affection aspects of morality is so important, and why care-based morality is not a threat to replace more impersonal duty ethics. The care-based ethic is fundamentally right: affection, caring, trusting,[2] and generous impulses are the moral foundation. And the tendency of reason-oriented ethical systems—whether Kantian or utilitarian[3]—to ignore that foundation has left an artificial ethics: a rationalist ethics that is well-suited for moral enhancement but crumbles underfoot when used as a moral foundation. Reason-based ethics reinforces rather than replaces care-based morality. The rules-reasons approach is an important means of extending and enhancing and sustaining moral behavior when affection has reached its limits, but the moral foundation—on which duty morality must build— remains the immediate nonreflective inclinations of care and affection:[4] inclinations rooted in biology, nurtured by direct and indirect reciprocity, and existing prior to rationality.

To see how reason can enhance (without supplanting) affection, consider an analogy with poetry. I may scribble some poetic lines, based on my mood or feelings: a verse pledging my love, or perhaps a celebration of beauty or an expression of despair. My untutored verses may be effective expressions even without the polished use of verse forms and without reflection on rules of poetic meter, but my poetry will likely improve if I learn to enhance it by deliberate thoughtful use of meter and rhythm and form. In like manner, my affectionate concern may prompt genuine moral behavior (and in some cases, more satisfactory moral behavior) even without reflection on rules of duty, but use of rules may enhance and strengthen moral practice. In both poetry and morality, the rules can also become an obsession and do more harm than good: the poet becomes affected and shallow, and her poetry becomes stylized and hollow; and analogously, the moralist can become so focused on rules that she mistakes them for the whole of morality and ignores the basic motives of affection and concern that drive morality—she has the form of morality, but her myopic focus on rules destroys the affectionate substance thereof. Along similar lines, one may know all the poetic metrical rules and forms but write shallow and trivial poetry, and one may know all the moral rules, yet be coldly uncaring and unhelpful. But when both function well, the reflective moral rules serve to enhance and strengthen and sustain the affectionate concerns on which they are based, just as the rules of meter and form serve to enhance poetic expression.

Rational-duty morality is an adaptive complement—rather than a competitor—to inclinations-caring morality, but it is still important to distinguish their functions and niches. Michael Ruse (1986, 241–242) suggests fixed limits beyond which our moral rules and reasoning cannot take us: for example, impassable biological limits on the utilitarian requirement to treat all persons equally, showing no favoritism to kin. Perhaps there are such limits. But because rules-duty morality (including such elaborate systems as utilitarianism) developed to *extend* the limits of affection and sympathy, it is impossible to predict the scope of such development on the basis of biological inclinations. Such rule-systems are a special enhancement of animal morality, and it remains an empirical question how far they can push morality. Not very far, it may appear; but we've only started trying. And here data from animal studies is of limited help, since this is a special rule-following adaptation not available to the morality of nonhuman animals. Biology—as vital as it is to our deep understanding of morality—can no more predict the development of rule-aided morality than it can predict what metrical forms future poetry might take. (That is not to suggest, of course, that the writing of poetry is some mystical and inexplicable act of "miraculous creativity"; rather, the combination of cultural and rule-following and linguistic and biological influences make the process too complex to be fully explained or predicted in terms of natural selection.)

On the basis of his meticulous and insightful primate studies, ethologist Frans de Waal justly criticizes moral philosophers for neglecting the animal roots of human moral behavior and overemphasizing reflective rule-following. But when he disparages some moral ideals (such as Peter Singer's ideal of an ever-extending circle of moral concern), de Waal fails to give full consideration to the special adaptive powers of moral rules and moral reasoning:

> The ideal of human brotherhood is unrealistic in that it fails to distinguish between these innermost and outermost circles of obligation. . . . If altruism evolved because of a need to cooperate against hostile forces, solidarity with what is close against what is distant is an integral part. (de Waal 1996, 214)

No doubt one of the forces pushing altruism was "a need to cooperate against hostile forces," but that does not settle the question of how far the altruistic affections can be extended by means of rules and reflection. Obviously not to the extent of eliminating the sympathetic affections in which such altruism is rooted; but whether such sympathy must remain localized and locked within an "us-against-them" form, or whether the use of rules and imaginative sympathy and processes of reflective universalization might push sympathetic affection beyond such barriers: that is an issue that remains to be resolved. Biologists and ethologists are no more entitled to pronounce fixed and impassable limits (prior to actual study of what rules and reflection can do in shaping and reshaping altruistic affections) than are philosophers. Biology has a great deal to teach us about morality, but biological studies cannot dictate in advance the range of moral development that is possible by use of reflective techniques that cannot be "biologicized." Nonetheless, however far such rational rule-following enhancement propels morality, human morality remains rooted in moral sentiments we share with other animals.

## Why Be Moral?

Our moral core is not built on social contracts, nor is it an objective truth discovered through special (exclusively human) deliberative powers. Recognizing the nonobjective animal-sentiments core of morality does not undermine morality, nor shake our commitment to the values we hold. To the contrary, it offers better guidance to how such basic value inclinations can be enhanced and extended, and how that vital sympathetic moral nucleus can be strengthened and sustained. And it helps resolve another ethical quandary: one that can challenge and perhaps even weaken our deep moral commitments. Moral philosophers often puzzle—and invite students to share our puzzlement—over the question of "Why should I be moral?" A variety of answers are offered, but they all seem slippery and ultimately unsatisfactory. And to the degree that they fail to rationally satisfy, they invite skepticism concerning basic moral commitments. I have no solid *reasons* for being moral, rather than being a free rider or a clever shirker. So perhaps morality is a sham, a clever ploy to take advantage of the gullible followers of morality: well, better to be the shearer than the sheep; so much for morality, let the devil take the hindmost.

But the problem is in the question: *Why* be moral? That is a subtly loaded question, that requires us to look for *reasons.* The embedded assumption is that if moral behavior is worthwhile for us, we must be able to give good *reasons* for *choosing* a moral life. That assumption makes sense in the rationalistic Platonic world, or perhaps within a theological framework in which humans are special separate rational creatures: we should act morally because it is in keeping with our distinctive nature, and part of our Creator's purpose for our lives. But if we have no such framework for supporting a rationally or theologically prescribed moral life, then raising the question soon leads to severe problems. After all, if the question is taken seriously, then a moral answer cannot be proposed without begging the question: You should be moral because it is morally good to be moral; that is no more satisfactory than saying you should believe in God because God commands it.

If we seek self-interested reasons that can answer "Why be moral?" we encounter other problems. First, if you regard acting morally (in a manner that takes into consideration the interests and feelings of others, and does not exclusively seek your own benefits) as simply one option, with a totally self-centered amoral life as another viable alternative, then it is quite difficult to offer you good reasons for being moral. Of course we can give good reasons for *appearing* to be moral, in order to gain the social benefits that accrue to that appearance; but it is much more difficult to give reasons why you should genuinely pursue a moral life, rather than a moral fraud that takes every possible immoral exploitative advantage. There are traditional attempts to prove that such a calculating immoralist would not be happy—your conscience will bother you, your life will require constant deception, you will cut yourself off from any genuine relations (you hide your real motives, so no one can care for you as you actually are)—but if you are the sort of person who can genuinely consider a life of systemic immorality as a livable possibility, then probably such concerns will not weigh heavily on you.

Second, and more basically, giving nonmoral reasons for why you are better off acting morally seems to undercut the entire enterprise of justifying morality. After all, if our reasons for acting morally are that we will gain more for ourselves (whether honor on Earth or glory in Heaven), then it is not at all clear that we have justified morality. If I perform a kind deed only for hope of reward or fame, then the moral worth of the deed is called into question. If you live a "moral" life strictly for your own calculated selfish benefit, then the very morality of that life likewise becomes doubtful. (A "moral agent" who acts generously only after calculating how he or she individually will benefit has a very thin claim on morality.) So *moral* reasons for "Why be moral" beg the question, while nonmoral reasons miss the mark. Moral life lacks a rational foundation, and thus questions and doubts arise that can lead to moral skepticism.

Seeking reasons for "why I should be moral" stems from the tradition that regards human behavior as special and distinct because humans alone act for *reasons*. The proper response to "Why be moral?" is not a quest for reasons to prop up allegiance to morality; rather, the answer is much more basic: If you really have to ask, you'll never understand. If a life lived without regard for the interests and welfare of others is a real option for you, then you lack the essential *nonrational* underpinnings for moral life: the feelings of concern and affection for others that are the foundation on which morality rests. If you have such motives, then "Why be moral?" seems a silly question, on a par with "Why love your children?" (It is certainly possible to raise questions about such affections, as it is to raise questions concerning elements of our moral life. It might be argued—very implausibly— that strong affection for one's children is too narrow and cuts one off from more universal concerns; or one might even argue that such affection is misplaced, since your children will some-day "turn on you." In like manner, it is possible to challenge par-ticular moral commitments, arguing that they cannot withstand close scrutiny, and should be displaced. But such challenges notwithstanding, it is still the case that I do not love my children from any *reasons*, and typically neither is my commitment to morality itself—as opposed to some particular item of moral belief—rationally founded.)

Living a moral life (not a *saintly* life, necessarily, nor even a morally exemplary life; but a *moral* life) is simply part of the way you live, and you cannot seriously entertain renouncing such a life. One might toy with the idea, as I might fantasize about abandoning my family for tropical island hedonism; but that is not a genuinely live option for me, anymore than is a life that renounces moral concerns. Of course under severe psy-chological or societal duress, my deep moral inclinations might erode; the fact that I cannot now give up morality does not imply that it could never happen. Still, for most of us life with-out morality is not a genuine possibility, and the question of "Why should I be moral?" is a misleading philosophical exercise rather than a serious question. On the other hand, for those who genuinely need some reasons that would convince them to be moral, it is doubtful that any will work. They lack the basic motivations that must be present in order for morality to be appealing.

In rare cases the question "Why be moral?" may be gen-uine: Kant may have been such a special exception. When he speaks of one who "is by temperament cold and indifferent to the sufferings of others perhaps because he is provided with special gifts of patience and fortitude," Kant is apparently indulging in self-congratulation; if so, his classic attempt to base morality purely on reason is an effort to fuel his own emo-tionally impoverished moral life:

> To be kind where one can is duty, and there are, moreover, many persons so sympathetically constituted that without any motive of vanity or selfishness they find an inner satisfaction in spreading joy and rejoice in the contentment of others which they have made possible. But I say that, however dutiful and amiable it may be, that kind of action has no true moral worth. It is on a level with other inclinations. . . . For the maxim lacks the moral import of an action done not from inclination but from duty. . . . If nature has put little sympathy in the heart of

> a man, and if he, though an honest man, is by temperament cold and indifferent to the sufferings of others perhaps because he is provided with special gifts of patience and fortitude, and expects or even requires that others should have the same— and such a man would certainly not be the meanest product of nature—would not he find in himself a source from which to give himself a far higher worth than he could have got by having a good-natured temperament? . . . [I]t is just here that the worth of the character is brought out, which is morally and incomparably the highest of all: he is beneficent not from inclination but from duty. (1785/1949, 60)

If nature (and nurture) "has put little sympathy in the heart of a man," then that individual might (as Kant apparently did) follow rules of duty as a special challenge: the struggle to follow such rules stringently and steadfastly, even against one's inclinations, becomes a point of pride and satisfaction (not to mention a source of honor and reward from the community). In similar manner, a distance runner or mountain climber might take pride in conquering her suffering and fears, even though the running or climbing are not (at least initially) in themselves a source of satisfaction. So it might be possible for someone (like Kant) to adhere to moral rules, while feeling no moral inclinations. But that will be a very uncommon phenomenon, certainly not the process by which morality is typically practiced by humans and other animals.

It is fortunate that Kant's is a rare means of being moral, since it yields a rather shabby moral life. In the first place, if your "moral behavior" is strictly and entirely guided by dutiful obligation, then your moral acts of kindness may not bring much satisfaction to the objects of your moral ministrations. Furthermore, such rule-driven morality is not likely to be enthusiastic nor polished nor effective—nor enduring. Kant's own moral behavior may be a case in point. Rae Langton (1992) discusses a woman who had carefully studied Kant's philosophy, and during a period of despair wrote to Kant for moral counsel and consolation. Kant (as Langton convincingly describes their exchange) failed to understand her quandary and ultimately treated her as merely a moral object lesson from whose experiences others might gain moral edification. In the performance of such basic moral acts as kindness and consolation, diligent but nonsympathetic duty-following is likely to prove inadequate.

It is true that should sorrow or exhaustion or stress threaten one's moral sympathies, then (as noted in chapter 10) humans may use moral rules and principles and reasoning to sustain or revive their moral commitments. But to suppose that "rules of duty" can *by themselves* hold our moral lives on a steadier course than can moral sentiments *aided* by such rules is to intellectualize morality into something uniquely human but also implausible and ineffective.

So leading a moral life is not basically a matter of finding the right *reasons* to be moral (and then seeking *motives* for following those rational principles). Nor is it a matter of stark *choice*, in which we choose our moral goods to pursue and follow them through heroic acts of will. Moral commitment is neither breast-beating, soul-wrenching existential ultimate choice nor choice of more modest proportions. It is not a choice at all. Life without morality is simply not a live option for most people. The idea that (without basic rational moral objectivity) there must be a radical choice of a moral (as opposed to an amoral or immoral) life grows from the same roots as the notion that there must be supportive *reasons* for living morally. Morality must be something distinctively human, something that sets us uniquely apart from the natural world. Making morality purely rational is one way of accomplishing that; radical choices that separate us from the natural world and its influences is another. Neither is plausible. We don't reason our way to our basic moral commitments, nor do we choose them. We no more choose to be moral than we choose to love our children.

We neither rationally derive nor existentially choose our basic moral inclinations. That does not, however, imply that morality cannot stand rational scrutiny. When we think about it, we are glad that we are moral animals—though we did not become moral animals through thinking about it, and we ultimately cannot give *reasons* for being moral. In similar fashion, our affection for our loved ones resulted neither from reason nor choice, but should we reflect on those affections, we do not reject them as irrational or repulsive (unless, perhaps, we are pure Kantians who long to be free of affection in order to glory in ascetically dutiful moral triumphs).

It is also possible to reflect on our moral inclinations (as well as our affections) and disapprove of some. In T. S. Eliot's phrase from *Four Quartets*, reflection may reveal harmful, hasty, or even vicious acts "which once you took for exercise of

virtue." What I once considered virtuous or even righteous retribution is now seen as unfair and unjust; my treatment of
other animals, once regarded as morally neutral, is now considered morally wrong. But reason has no monopoly in the revision of moral inclinations and judgments, since such changes
can occur without rational reflection. Visiting an abattoir—or
watching *Bambi*, for that matter—can modify my moral perspective; and racist inclinations—even a racist morality—might
be changed through reflections on justice from behind a Rawl-
sian veil of ignorance, but also by immediate broadening nonreflective close encounters with warm and generous persons
from other ethnic and racial groups.

Just as I can revise my moral views (through reflection and
otherwise), I can also revise my affections: I can, for example,
decide that my affection is misplaced (this person is a schemer,
not a real friend). But the possibility of such revisions of affections—*sometimes* on the basis of rational reflection—does not
mean that *non*reflective affections are not genuine and deep,
nor does it imply that affections can be entirely supported by
reason. One "falls" in love, typically; it is not a rational process.
Likewise, the fact that moral inclinations are sometimes use-
fully revised through reflection does not imply that *non*reflective
moral inclinations are less moral or less profound, nor that they
can be built on a foundation of rationality.

## The Role of Moral Philosophy

Moral reasoning and moral philosophy do not guide us to
the fundamental right reasons for a moral life and cannot provide the essential sympathetic foundation for morality; still,
there remains much for moral reasoning to do. As already
noted, there is the important work of enhancing and strengthening and sustaining and extending—and in some cases, modifying and controlling—the inclinations and affections at the
roots of morality. That is a limited function, but a vitally important one. For example, there may be a natural strike-back, retributive impulse; but reflection can keep it in check and even
modify the inclination itself (with the aid of other inclinations
that reflection enhances). Again, our species may have a natural inclination to favor those who physically resemble us over
those of marked physical differences. We know to what terrible

racist ends such inclinations can lead, and reason can aid in modifying those inclinations: she happens to look different from me, but we have similar feelings, motives, affections, and interests; and it is *unfair* to treat her shabbily. (In such cases reasoning can strengthen inclinations toward extended kindness and help to check competing motives.) Moral reasoning is valuable in such circumstances, but even there it holds no monopoly. Racist sentiments that propped up slavery may have been modified by reflection; but Harriet Beecher Stowe's sentimental *Uncle Tom's Cabin* did more than Kant's rationalistic *Metaphysics of Morals* to change those attitudes. Reason has an important role in improving, strengthening, and extending moral inclinations; but so do novels, poems, and paintings.

Moral reasoning is important, but it is also important to recognize the limits of what moral reasoning and moral philosophy can accomplish, so they will not be called upon to perform tasks beyond their capacities. In particular, moral reasoning—and instruction in moral philosophy—cannot produce moral individuals. An alarming number of physicians and executives and lawyers and other professionals abuse their privileges and powers to exploit others, and so we prescribe an ethics course. Such courses have their uses. But when ethics courses—whether ethical theory or applied ethics—are prescribed as the moral corrective for professionals who abuse positions of privilege to grossly mistreat and exploit vulnerable patients and clients, then an ethics course is the wrong medicine. What is lacking is not the refinement and enhancement of sound generous moral inclinations; rather, it is that foundation itself that is absent, and reason cannot supply what is missing. Those who feel a basic inclination toward respect and kindness can gain moral benefit from a course in bioethics: the course can strengthen those moral impulses, provide rules that sustain them through stress, make students more keenly aware of the feelings and interests of those with whom they deal professionally, and make moral students aware of subtle and remote effects they had not considered. But if a student regards patients as simply the means to riches, as an inconvenience that must be dealt with, as beneath the serious consideration of his or her high status, then an ethics course will not correct that problem.

To the contrary, the ethics course may exacerbate it, by showing the student how to accommodate the minimum rules and formulas of professional standards without having the affective substance that gives them life and makes them work. Such physicians "do the consent form" but fail to genuinely respect the patient's concerns and interests. If the foundational moral affections and sympathies are missing, then ethical reasoning—which works to extend and enhance and sustain such basic moral motives—has nothing on which to build.

That does not mean we must despair of those who lack basic moral motives; rather, it means that efforts to develop their moral foundations cannot be based on reason. It also does not imply that we should subject them to *Clockwork Orange* vicious coercive "therapy." Affectionate care can be nurtured, and coercion is not the best path to such basic care development. Neither is philosophy, for that matter—though it is an improvement over coercion. A loving family, supportive community, generous friends—and perhaps heart-warming stories— are better sources. If those forces have been absent, or have somehow failed to establish the essential roots of sympathy and affection from which morality grows, it will be a profound challenge to remedy the lack in an adult. But that challenge cannot be met by either philosophy or coercion.

Philosophy has long since stepped down from its exalted position as queen of the sciences, but in ethics there has been greater reluctance to relinquish the throne. Recognizing that philosophical reflective reasoning does not map the one true path to either morality or autonomy replaces the royal privileges with a more cooperative and democratic spirit. The conditions under which moral inclinations and autonomy develop and flourish can be studied by biologists and sociologists, psychologists and historians. Moral philosophers may enrich and refine our moral inclinations—but so also can biologists and psychologists, novelists and artists, friends and lovers. Philosophical reflection is an enhancer rather than a creator or legislator of moral inclinations, and reflection enriches rather than transcends biology. Rational reflection plays a less exalted but more effective role, while nonreflective affectionate caring remains the vital center of animal moral life.

# Notes

## Chapter Two

1. Libertarians have typically treated autonomy-as-alternatives as a wonderful mystery: Richard Taylor states that "the conception of a thing's being 'within one's power' or 'up to him' seems to defy analysis or definition altogether" (1963, 57), and Roderick Chisholm asserts that ". . . we have a prerogative which some would attribute only to God: each of us, when we really act, is a prime mover unmoved" (1975, 395). Robert Kane (1985) is a noteworthy exception. His unique version of the libertarian rejection of determinism incorporates randomness but scrupulously avoids mystery, while attempting to preserve moral responsibility.

2. Gerald Dworkin finds that not at all obvious. To the contrary, Dworkin insists on the possibility of autonomous slaves, and would not agree that such a result reveals a fatal flaw in autonomy-as-authenticity:

> In my conception, the autonomous person can be a tyrant or a slave, a saint or sinner, a rugged individualist or a champion of fraternity, a leader or a follower. (1988, 29)

This might be interpreted as an autonomous slave autonomously choosing a life of slavery (or of soldierly regimentation, to take another of Dworkin's provocative examples) from among several alternatives; but then having chosen slavery, the slave is no longer autonomous. One autonomously chooses to be a slave, but one is not an ongoing autonomous slave. But it is doubtful that Dworkin would accept this: for Dworkin, the slave who wants to be a slave really is an ongoing autonomous slave, even in the absence of other options or possibilities of escape.

3. Marvin Zuckerman (1983) notes interesting studies of similar phenomena:

167

Whether they "need" to or not, species other than human do show spontaneous variation in instrumental behavior (Glanzer 1953; Tolman 1925), prefer stimuli of some complexity to simpler stimuli (Sackett 1972), and approach and investigate novel stimuli in spite of their initial fears of such stimuli (Suomi & Harlow 1976).

4. Wolf has a possible answer: if keeping options open (by means of occasionally choosing a path other than the one Reason selects as optimum) is the best means of ultimately discovering the full range of truth, then genuine Reason must recommend such options as truly Reasonable. Thus "any attempt to offer reasons for wanting to act against Reason will only show that the sense of Reason under attack is not the sense intended"(1990, 56). But such a response reduces to: the true path of the True and Good may involve following alternative paths. That does save the single-True-path-of-Reason model, but at the cost of making it vacuous. In sum, then, the Reason justification for single-path authenticity fails to either include or refute the strengths of autonomy-as-alternatives.

5. William A. Mason (1993, 25) notes as a basic observation (underlying his further research on dominance relations) that:

Primates generally act so as to maximize their personal freedom and mobility under demanding circumstances.

6. See Waller 1988; and Waller 1990.

7. Bernard Williams (1993, 154) notes that:

. . . being free stands opposed, above all, to being in someone's power; and the mark of that . . . is that my choices or opportunities are not merely limited . . . but that they are designedly and systematically limited, by another person who is shaping my actions to his intentions. To lack freedom is paradigmatically not simply to be short of choices, but to be subject to the will of another.

Certainly being subject to the power and manipulation of another is an exemplar of lost freedom; but rather than being the defining mark of loss of freedom, it is a special case of being (in Williams' phrase) "short of choices." Captain Ahab's terrible obsession with Moby Dick deprives him of options and of freedom, though not through the machinations of any person. And if I am trapped hand and foot in a rock slide, then my freedom is curtailed by this natural disaster and is not the result of humans' shaping or controlling me. (I may not feel personally demeaned and abused by the rock slide, as I may well feel if I am held fast by the intentionally cruel behavior of human captors; but my freedom—that is, my open options and choices—is equally lost in both cases.) In short, lacking freedom is indeed "simply to be short of choices"; human purposeful manipulation that deprives us of such choices is one of the most common—and painful—ways that choices are curtailed and freedom is destroyed, but it is not the only one.

8. Donald Campbell (1974) gives a superb account of how human intelligence, language, and social cooperation function as highly successful "vicarious locomotor devices": as further enhancements of exploratory processes starting with blind bodily overt movement and ranging through more efficient visual search to highly efficient language-enhanced socially vicarious exploration.

9. This is one of Gerald Dworkin's (1976, 25) many provocative examples.

## Chapter Three

1. Gerald Dworkin, for example, has written a powerful appeal for protecting the freedom and integrity of mental patients (Dworkin 1976).

2. For more details on the "willful" submissiveness of the dog that has learned helplessness in response to inescapable shock (and now refuses to attempt escape even when the shock is avoidable), see Seligman (1975).

3. William James (1897) develops this claim in passionate detail.

## Chapter Four

1. The assumption that moral responsibility is inseparable from autonomy is not quite universal among philosophers. Bernard Williams (1985/1995, 6, 9) asserts that we could keep "functioning psychological concepts of choice and intentional action" while dropping traditional notions of blame.

## Chapter Five

1. Arguments on why effort-making cannot establish moral responsibility are briefly discussed in chapter 8; for more extensive arguments, see Waller 1990, chapter 7.

2. Charles Taylor (1976, 299) describes the "depersonifying" effects of being denied such choices.

## Chapter Six

1. Lawrence Blum (1980, 188–190) is among the few philosophers who allow for moral behavior without moral responsibility. But even he seems to hold that the core of moral agency requires moral responsibility, though the more inclusive moral category of "moral being" does not.

2. I regard the question concerning virtue as simply the flip side of the vice question. That is the common view, but it is not quite universal. For an opposing perspective, see Susan Wolf 1980.

3. Herbert Morris (1968) and Andrew Oldenquist (1988) offer further noteworthy examples of the view that to deny someone's moral responsibility entails classifying that individual as so severely substandard as to be excluded from the moral community.

4. On this point, see Bernard Gert 1988, 214. Concerning the moral behavior of the "imbecilic and deranged," I maintain that the scope of their moral behavior is limited, but that they can behave morally. That issue is examined further in chapter 9.

5. Hospers allows only insignificant exceptions:

If people generally call most acts free, it is . . . through not knowing how large a proportion of our acts actually are compelled. Only the comparatively 'vanilla-flavored' aspects of our lives—such as our behavior toward people who don't really matter to us—are exempted from this rule. (Hospers 1952, 574)

6. Howard Hintz (1958) correctly notes that Hospers' view would undermine moral life; but the reason is because of Hospers' special (flaw-based) grounds for denial of moral responsibility, *not* because the denial of moral responsibility is itself damaging to morality.

7. See, for example, C. S. Lewis (1970), Andrew Oldenquist (1988, 467), and Jeffrie Murphy (1979, 109–110).

8. For insightful discussion of differing world views and "metaphilosophies," see Richard Double 1996.

9. See Waller 1988.

10. Of course—from this scientific naturalism perspective—there are causes for one's deliberations and reflections and choices; but while that undermines moral responsibility, it does not prevent one's deliberations and choices from being one's own, nor does it make such caused deliberations self-defeating. Of course, some think otherwise:

for examples, see Colson 1982; Eccles 1976, 101; Flew 1986; Hinman 1979a and 1979b, 294–295; Llewelyn 1966; MacIntyre 1957; and Wolf 1981, 397–399. For refutation of such claims see Churchland 1981; Dennett 1984, chap. 2; Skinner 1969, chaps. 6 and 8, and 1974, chaps. 7, 8, and 9; Toulmin 1970; Waller 1982 and 1985; and Williams 1985/1995, 9.

## Chapter Seven

1. In his influential account of the development of reciprocal altruism, Robert Trivers (1971) emphasizes the importance of aid in combat and defense.

2. This is not to suggest that morality did not originate until the emergence of monkeys and apes. If morality developed earlier, then some analogue of kin grooming probably played an essential role.

3. James Rachels (1991, 156–157) offers a particularly clear and compelling account of this process. Becker (1986, 91) notes that absence of reciprocity "would quite likely extinguish helping behavior." For a more extensive discussion, see Alexander 1987, especially chapter 2.

4. Trivers (1971) used the phrase "generalized reciprocity"; Alexander (1987, 119) prefers "indirect reciprocity."

5. Mackie, of course, does not offer this as an account of the development of objective morality, but rather as an account of why morality is thought and felt to be objective when in fact it is not.

6. At least it seems likely that a care-based system could flourish without moral responsibility judgments: there are no inherent contradictions or obvious fatal flaws in a care-based system without moral responsibility. Whether it would actually flourish is an empirical issue. Not that it's an empirical issue whether it is the right moral system; rather, it is an empirical, sociological, anthropological question whether such a system would function as an effective moral system for a community.

7. See Waller 1989.

8. On this point, see Mary Midgley's (1978, 117) insightful analysis.

9. Virginia Held (1990) elucidates the shared assumptions of these positions.

10. See, for example, Oldenquist 1988, 467.

11. These improved strategies might involve encouraging—even positively reinforcing, or "rewarding"—the development of virtue. But in the absence of moral responsibility, such promotion of virtue will not be done in ways that match or even approximate the rewards and punishments meted out by the principles of just deserts. For a more detailed discussion of why distributing benefits and rewards in accordance with "just deserts" is not the best means of shaping good behavior, see Waller 1989.

## Chapter Eight

1. Moritz Schlick (1939) claims that the educational-correctional function *is* the essence of moral responsibility. The question of who is morally responsible is simply a question of: where do we most effectively apply the sanctions? But that fails to justify anything even approximating "just deserts" and moral responsibility. The most effective behavior shaping may occur *before* the acts that we should like to modify (or prevent); and even after such acts, the optimum reinforcement pattern is more likely to be in sharp contrast to the demands of just deserts (see Waller 1989).

## Chapter Nine

1. Frans de Waal (1996, 210) makes a similar point:

A chimpanzee stroking and patting a victim of attack or sharing her food with a hungry companion shows attitudes that are hard to distinguish from those of a person picking up a crying child, or doing volunteer work in a soup kitchen. To classify the chimpanzee's behavior as based on instinct and the person's behavior as proof of moral decency is misleading, and probably incorrect. First of all, it is uneconomic in that it assumes different processes for similar behavior in two closely related species.

2. For example, Joseph Ellin states the standard view in his introductory ethics textbook: ". . . If you do not think about your values, then you are not moral even if you happen to have the correct values." (Ellin 1995, 295) This view has been dominant from Plato through Kant and remains the consensus among contemporary philosophers. There are, however, some noteworthy exceptions. Among the most forceful dissenters are Iris Murdoch (1971) and Lawrence Blum (1980).

3. Of course there is a "deeper" cause for such solicitude: the preservation of one's genetic legacy. But though that may be the ultimate cause, it does not alter or diminish the genuine selfless concern for the child. Genetic preservation may cause my love, but the rush to rescue is no less motivated by genuine love for the child. (Genetic preservation also fuels my sex drive, but my passion is not directed at the preservation of my genes.) Even if solicitude has its origins in "selfish genes," that does not diminish its genuine moral value. Frans de Waal (1996, 16–17) offers an apt analogy:

Even if a diamond owes its beauty to millions of years of crushing pressure, we rarely think of this fact when admiring the gem. So why should we let the ruthlessness of natural selection distract from the wonders it has produced? Humans and other animals have been endowed with a capacity for genuine love, sympathy, and care—a fact that can and will one day be fully reconciled with the idea that genetic self-promotion drives the evolutionary process.

4. A similar point is made by Lawrence Blum in his account of "direct altruism":

The direct altruism view means to express a kind of virtue which does not depend on moral reflectiveness or self-consciousness. It depends only on being responsive to the weal and woe of others. . . . The compassionate or kind person does not necessarily or typically act in order to be virtuous. . . . He need not *aim* at being kind or compassionate. . . . What is necessary is only that he aim to meet the other's need, relieve her suffering, etc. (1980, 100)

5. See, for example, Frans de Waal 1982, 207.

6. For further discussion of tropistic behavior and its implications, see Rachels 1990, 143–147.

7. This is an example of the confusions and complications that can grow in contexts of referential opacity; see Quine 1960.

8. Lawrence Blum (1980, 9–10) uses "altruism" in the sense of "a regard for the good of another person for his own sake, or conduct motivated by such a regard." As he notes, this usage does not require that altruism involve self-sacrifice. In most of the following discussion, I shall follow Blum's usage; however, the controversy in evolutionary biology concerning how an "altruistic" motive could take root and spread through natural selection involves the self-sacrificial sense of "altruism," and where that use is at issue it will be specified. But the difference between the two senses of "altruism" may not be as great as

it might immediately appear. My altruistic act of stopping to allow another motorist into a lane of traffic hardly qualifies as a heroic self-sacrificing act; nonetheless, such an altruistic tendency may still qualify as strong self-sacrificial altruism from the perspective of natural selection, since it does *marginally* reduce my reproductive fitness (this mild altruistic tendency slightly increases the amount of time I fritter away in traffic, thus slightly reducing the opportunities I—and my genes—have to "get ahead"). So the difference in forms of altruism may be more like points on a continuum than a clear and dramatic difference.

9. James Rachels (1990, 149–152) discusses this case. The original research reports are in Masserman, Wechkin, and Terris 1964; and Wechkin, Masserman, and Terris 1964.

10. We often prefer nondeliberative ethical behavior not only in the performance of virtuous acts, but also in the avoidance of vicious behavior. Bernard Williams offers the following illustration:

> An effective way for actions to be ruled out is that they never come into thought at all, and this is often the best way. One does not feel easy with the man who in the course of a discussion of how to deal with political or business rivals says, "Of course, we could have them killed, but we should lay that aside right from the beginning." It should never have come into his hands to be laid aside. (Williams 1985, 185)

11. If rule use were required for our best ethical behavior, that would make ethics a very unusual human enterprise. (Those who celebrate ethics as the activity that secures humans a special place apart from the natural world may view this as a benefit.) Typically we use rules to guide our clumsy early efforts, and once we master the skills, the rules are seldom considered. (This point is discussed, in a different context, by B. F. Skinner 1978, 12.) Instead of rule-following, the skilled behavior is shaped by its effects. The beginning violinist concentrates on her teacher's rules ("keep the wrist firm and the fingers relaxed"), but the polished player responds directly to her subtle effects on her instrument. In like manner, the individual who must rehearse the rules in order to act morally is less likely to be a polished moral actor. The morally skilled respond to subtle complex social environments and to the effects of their behavior on their changing environments, and heavy reliance on rules is likely to be an encumbrance. (Perhaps that accounts for Kant's moral clumsiness; see Langton 1994.)

12. Lawrence A. Blum notes that emotions of sympathy and compassion (without the aid of reason) "are not essentially transient, weak and capricious, but rather are able to withstand changes in mood and

impulse, and can motivate us to act contrary to our inclinations and interests." (1980, 30)

13. Bernard Williams (1965/1973, 227) makes this point with his customary clarity:

> . . . I suspect it to be true of moral, as it certainly is of factual, convictions that we cannot take very seriously a profession of them if we are given to understand that the speaker has just *decided* to adopt them. The idea that people decide to adopt their moral principles seems to me a myth, a psychological shadow thrown by a logical distinction; and if someone did claim to have done this, I think one would be justified in doubting either the truth of what he said or the reality of those moral principles. We see a man's genuine convictions as coming from somewhere deeper in him than that. . . .

14. Some compatibilists will say that she is morally responsible no matter how she got that way. That seems implausible to me, but it doesn't matter here. If one takes that view, then nonreflective genetically generous Joyce should be counted as morally responsible; and so such compatiblists cannot claim that nonreflective Joyce is nonmoral because nonresponsible.

15. If one follows the traditional Humean compatibilist line—the causal source of one's virtuous or vicious character is irrelevent to one's moral responsibility—then obviously the demand for moral responsibility cannot be used to support a *causal* requirement of rational reflection for moral character.

16. Thus one might count both rational and nonrational animals as moral without holding them morally responsible.

## Chapter Ten

1. As Frans de Waal states:

> Aid to others in need would never be internalized as a duty without the fellow-feeling that drives people to take an interest in one another. Moral sentiments came first; moral principles, second. (de Waal 1996, 87; see also de Waal 1996, 45)

2. Mary Midgley (1978, 167–168) notes that the social contract myth misleads because it suggests that rationality made social cooperation possible, while in fact cooperative behavior was a precondition of the development of rational processes. However, Midgley (1994, 173) regards such rational development (together with cooperative inclina-

tions) as essential for morality, and thus denies that animals lacking human rational capacities can act morally.

3. Neven Sesardic (1995) develops an account of moral development that is somewhat similar to Alexander's, but Alexander's has the advantage of allowing morality and rationality to develop together. Sesardic requires high-level cognition as a starting condition for morality, and thus morality must emerge at a late cognitive stage with a very thin developmental history. Sesardic discusses a wide range of biological work on the evolution of altruism, but makes no reference to Richard Alexander's (1979, 1982, 1985, 1987) extensive and influential work in the area.

Though I find Alexander's account more plausible, Sesardic's subtle and thoughtful article offers a cogent and innovative explanation of how a genuine tendency toward cooperative altruistic behavior might be fitness decreasing on each occasion when it is manifested, yet the possession of that cooperative disposition nonetheless be fitness increasing for the individual (Sesardic 1995, 150).

4. Since kin and reciprocal altruism both are fitness enhancing for the genes of the altruistic individual, Sesardic does not count them as genuine altruism.

5. Frans de Waal (1996, 78) describes the limited but important role of reason:

> Cognitive evolution does not invent new categories of behavior. It works with, rather than replaces, the ancient emotional infrastructure, transforming it by an ever-greater understanding on the part of the actors.

6. Peter Singer (1981, 139) also emphasizes the adaptive advantages of reason. But rather than viewing rationality as useful for (among other things) enhancing moral behavior, Singer regards reason as so beneficial that rationality continues to be selected for despite the fact that rationality carries with it the individually disadvantageous baggage of extended altruism (since reason "brings with it an appreciation of the reasons for extending to strangers the concern we feel for our kin and our friends"). (Colin McGinn 1979, goes even further. McGinn argues that since evolutionary processes could not possibly result in altruistic behavior, the only plausible account of its development must involve the cognitive recognition of true moral facts as an inescapable side effect of the benefits of developing rationality.) But Singer's supposition that such moral extensions of altruism would be selectively disadvantageous is implausible. Groups made up of individuals that shared strong intragroup inclinations toward cooperation and mutual support would be more likely to prosper (group selection remains, of course, a matter of controversy; some recent defenses of group selection include D. S. Wil-

son 1983, and Wilson and Sober 1994); and individuals and groups that are strongly inclined toward intragroup cooperation will possess inclinations of altruism, cooperation, and conflict resolution that facilitate extending cooperative behavior to other groups. And certainly groups that were able to peacefully resolve some potential conflicts with neighboring groups would enjoy substantive advantages. In short, if nonrational inclinations can account for the development, spread, and survival of cooperative intragroup behavior, there is reason to believe that similar nonrational processes could establish intergroup cooperation. Rationality could enhance that process, certainly; but rationality need not be a *condition* of—rather than an important enhancer of—such moral behavior as extended altruism.

7. Povinelli and Godfrey (1993) argue that ethical systems require the development and attribution of values and the sharing and communication of such values. In order for ethical systems to develop, there must be second-order attribution of values as well as (they think likely) both active teaching and use of language. These are stiff requirements, which only the human species can meet. Thus ethical systems—complete with rules and ethical training and deliberation—belong only to humans, and only humans enjoy the moral advantages (and disadvantages) of such systems. But even if Povinelli and Godfrey are correct about ethical *systems*, it does not follow that members of other species cannot act morally. One can act morally (as the example of Huck Finn indicates) without sharing or communicating a moral system. It may well be that to *evaluate* behavior as moral or immoral, or to communicate such evaluations, will require knowledge of ethical systems; it does not follow that such systemic knowledge is necessary for moral behavior.

8. Higher-order reflection on desires and character is often seen by philosophers as the key to autonomy, responsibility, and genuine moral action: see, for example, Gerald Dworkin 1988; Harry G. Frankfurt 1971 and 1969; and Charles Taylor 1976.

9. Obviously the strengthening and extending of altruism and concern is not the whole of morality. As Alan Gewirth (1993, 248) notes, ethics is not solely a matter of consideration of interests of others; there are also questions of whose interests and which interests ought to be favorably considered (questions of individual rights, just distribution, and genuine conflicts of interest). See also Murphy 1982, 85.

## Chapter Eleven

1. For a similar view (with somewhat greater emphasis on culture as the source of the autonomy of human ethical systems), see Ayala 1987.

2. Frans de Waal (1982, 112) notes that adult male chimpanzees often live together in groups, reconcile their conflicts, and "see themselves as comrades." In contrast, adult male gorillas and orangutans tolerate no rivals "and their fights will end in a bloodbath." As de Waal comments: "it is of course this aspect of chimpanzee society which makes it so much more readily understandable to us than the social structures of other great ape societies." Along similar lines, while the morality of gorillas may not be totally beyond our comprehension, chimpanzee morality is much more accessible.

3. Jeffrie G. Murphy (1982, 99, 109) suggests a similar role for basic biologically grounded value commitments.

4. This leaves room for a limited sort of morality justification: it may still be possible to justify our moral commitments as *not* being *irrational*; or even stronger, to justify our moral commitments as reasonable and acceptable and *approved* by us in the full understanding of their causes, conditions, and consequences. Richmond Campbell's recent work is an elegant and cogent demonstration of how such justification can be compatible with Darwinism; see particularly Campbell 1988, and also Campbell 1984, and Campbell 1996.

5. Richmond Campbell offers a generous interpretation of Ruse's claim that we are genetically compelled to accept the moral objectivity illusion. Campbell suggests that what Ruse really has in mind is comparable to the compelling illusion of a 3–D movie, which remains effective even when we know it is not literally real.

> Likewise when one witnesses gratuitous cruelty, one may feel that there is a wrongness about what is done which exists independently of one's judgment, even though one might know "in one's head" (supposing that Ruse is right) that no such objective wrongness really exists. (Campbell 1996, 23–24)

This is a generous interpretation, but it makes Ruse's claim somewhat weaker, and I am not sure that Ruse would accept it. In any case, my argument is that even this more modest illusion is not necessary.

## Chapter Twelve

1. A similar argument for moral realism, based on analogous scientific value presuppositions, has recently been developed by Lowell Kleiman (1989).

2. This example is taken from Herbert Feigl 1950, 135. The nonobjectivism put forward here was greatly influenced by that article,

as well as by Feigl 1952. For a defense of this view against earlier attacks, see Waller 1986.

3. Bernard Williams believes that "the project of giving to ethical life an objective and determinate grounding in considerations about human nature is not . . . very likely to succeed." (1985, 153) But he considers it "at any rate a comprehensible project, and . . . the only intelligible form of ethical objectivity at the reflective level," and he makes some remarks concerning the boundaries of the project:

> We should notice, first, how it would have to be human beings that were primarily the subject of our ethics, since it would be from their nature that its conclusions would have to be drawn. Here this project joins hands with contractualism, in seeing other animals as outside the primary constituency of ethics, and at most beneficiaries of it. . . . (Williams 1985, 153–154)

Williams is right that such an ethical objectivity project makes humans the sole subject of ethics. Even within those limits the project is unlikely to succeed, but the drawing of that exclusive boundary undermines the project from the outset. A system that maximizes all and only human flourishing—to the exclusion of all other species—is no more a legitimate claimant for the title of objective ethics than would be a view based exclusively on the flourishing of all white males, or all Italians, or all mammals, or all aardvarks. "This is the optimum moral system for all human beings; but is it really in the best interests of all sentient creatures?" If such questions can be ruled out as illegitimate, that shows the provincialism of this approach, not its objectivity. Excluding animals from ethics makes it easier to get *closer* to some limited form of moral objectivism, in terms of "what works best for social human beings"; but the exclusion is illegitimate, as is the supposed moral objectivity constructed on its basis.

4. Nietzsche (infamously) champions such values; more recently such values have been espoused by such "deep ecologists" as J. Baird Callicott 1980. Frans de Waal (1996, 183–186) argues that some aggression and conflict is useful in primate societies, but he is certainly no champion of conflict as a basic value. De Waal regards limited aggression as a means of establishing order and thus lessening overall conflict, and he views reconciliation and compassion as vital valuable resources for ameliorating conflict and aggression.

## Chapter Thirteen

1. Lawrence Blum (1980, 143) notes that for the recipient of such a dutiful visit "the good to her of the dutiful visit will be mitigated by

her discomfort, anger, or disappointment" when she realizes that the visit is motivated by duty rather than personal concern. Along similar lines, Philip Mercer (1972, 102) notes "the interesting fact that most people would prefer to receive the help of someone who helped them because he sympathized with them rather than the help of someone who helped them because he thought it was his duty to do so."

2. See Baier 1985.

3. As Virginia Held (1990) has noted, the usually contrasted Kantian and utilitarian approaches to ethics share an assumption that reason must be given priority in morality.

4. That is, such care and affection forms the foundation for the morality I favor, and that (I hope) you favor, and that (I trust) is the predominant form of morality among humans. As noted in the previous chapter, it is not the only possible form of morality; one might instead base morality (as Nietzsche did) on the aggressive and selfish motives we also find deep in ourselves.

# References

Alexander, Richard. 1987. *The Biology of Moral Systems*. New York: Aldine de Gruyter.

Alexander, Richard. 1985. A biological interpretation of moral systems. *Zygon* 20:3–20.

Alexander, Richard. 1982. Biology and the moral paradoxes. In *Law, Biology, and Culture: The Evolution of Law*, ed. M. Gruter and P. Bohannan, 101–110. Santa Barbara, Calif.: Ross-Erikson.

Alexander, Richard. 1979. Evolution, social behavior, and ethics. In *The Foundations of Ethics and its Relationship to Science. IV. Knowing and Valuing: The Search for Common Roots*, ed. H. T. Engelhardt and D. Callahan, 124–155. Hastings-on-Hudson, N.Y.: Hastings Institute.

Ayala, F. J. 1987. The biological roots of morality. *Biology and Philosophy* 2:235–252.

Ayer, A. J. 1952. *Language, Truth, and Logic*. New York: Dover.

Baier, Annette C. 1985. What do women want in a moral theory? *Nous* 19:53–63.

Batson, C. Daniel. 1991. *The Altruism Question: Toward a Social-Psychological Answer*. Hillsdale, N.J.: Lawrence Erlbaum Associates, Publishers.

Becker, Lawrence C. 1986. *Reciprocity*. London: Routledge & Kegan Paul.

Bennett, Jonathan. 1980a. Accountability. In *Philosophical Subjects*, ed. Zak van Straaten, 14–47. Oxford: Clarendon Press.

Bennett, Jonathan. 1980b. Towards a theory of punishment. *Philosophic Exchange* 3:43–54.

Bennett, Jonathan. 1974. The conscience of Huckleberry Finn. *Philosophy* 49:123–134.

Blum, Lawrence A. 1980. *Friendship, Altruism and Morality*. London: Routledge & Kegan Paul.

Boyd, Richard N. 1988. How to be a moral realist. In *Essays on Moral Realism*, ed. Geoffrey Sayre-McCord, 181–228. Ithaca, N.Y.: Cornell University Press.

Bradie, Michael. 1994. *The Secret Chain: Evolution and Ethics*. Albany: State University of New York Press.

Callicott, J. Baird. 1980. Animal liberation: A triangular affair. *Environmental Ethics* 2:311–338.

Campbell, C. A. 1957. *On Selfhood and Godhood*. London: George Allen & Unwin.

Campbell, Donald T. 1974. Evolutionary epistemology. In *The Philosophy of Karl Popper*, ed. Paul A. Schilpp. LaSalle, Ill.: Open Court.

Campbell, Richmond. 1996. Can biology make ethics objective? *Biology and Philosophy* 11:21–31.

Campbell, Richmond. 1988. Socially generated moral justification. In *Ethics and Justification*, ed. Douglas Odegard, 241–255. Edmonton, Alberta: Academic Printing & Publishing.

Campbell, Richmond. 1984. Sociobiology and the possibility of ethical naturalism. In *Morality, Reason and Truth*, ed. David Copp and David Zimmerman, 270–296. Totowa, N.J.: Rowman & Allanheld, Publishers.

Chisholm, Roderick. 1964/1982. Human freedom and the self, The Lindley Lecture, University of Kansas. Reprinted in *Free Will*, ed. Gary Watson, 24–35. Oxford: Oxford University Press, 1982.

Churchland, Patricia. 1981. Is determinism self-refuting? *Mind* 40: 99–101.

Colson, Daniel D. 1982. The transcendental argument against determinism: A challenge yet unmet. *Southern Journal of Philosophy* 20:15–24.

Copleston, F. C. 1948/1965. The Existence of God: A Debate. Originally broadcast by BBC. Printed in *A Modern Introduction to Philosophy*, rev. ed., ed. Paul Edwards and Arthur Pap. New York: The Free Press.

Darwin, Charles. 1871. *The Descent of Man, and Selection in Relation to Sex.* London: John Murray.

Dennett, Daniel. 1984. *Elbow Room.* Cambridge, Mass.: MIT Press.

Dostoyevsky, F. 1864/1961. *Notes from Underground.* Trans. Andrew R. MacAndrew. New York: New American Library, 1961.

Double, Richard. 1996. *Metaphilosophy and Free Will.* New York: Oxford University Press.

Double, Richard. 1991. *The Non-Reality of Free Will.* New York: Oxford University Press.

Dworkin, Gerald. 1988. *The Theory and Practice of Autonomy.* Cambridge: Cambridge University Press.

Dworkin, Gerald. 1976. Autonomy and behavior control. *Hastings Center Report* 6:23–28.

Eccles, John C. 1976. Brain and free will. In *Consciousness and the Brain: A Scientific and Philosophical Inquiry,* ed. Gordon Globus, Grover Maxwell, and Irwin Savodnik, 101–121. New York: Plenum Press.

Ellin, Joseph. 1995. *Morality and the Meaning of Life.* Fort Worth, Texas: Harcourt Brace.

Feigl, Herbert. 1952. Validation and vindication. In *Readings in Ethical Theory,* ed. C. Sellars and J. Hospers, 667–680. New York: Appleton-Century-Crofts.

Feigl, Herbert. 1950. 'De principiis non disputandum . . . ?' On the meaning and the limits of justification. In *Philosophical Analysis,* ed. Max Black, 113–147. Ithaca, New York: Cornell University Press.

Flew, Antony. 1986. Rationality and unnecessitated choice. In *Naturalism and Rationality,* ed. Newton Garver and Peter H. Hare, 41–51. Buffalo, N.Y.: Prometheus Books.

Frankfurt, Harry G. 1975. Three concepts of free action. *Aristotelian Society Proceedings* Supplementary Vol. 49: 113–25.

Frankfurt, Harry G. 1971. Freedom of the will and the concept of a person. *The Journal of Philosophy* 68:5–20.

Frankfurt, Harry G. 1969. Alternate possibilities and moral responsibility. *The Journal of Philosophy* 66:829–839.

Gaylin, Willard. 1982. *The Killing of Bonnie Garland.* New York: Simon and Schuster.

Gert, Bernard. 1988. *Morality: A New Justification of the Moral Rules.* New York: Oxford University Press.

Gewirth, Alan. 1993. How ethical is evolutionary ethics? In *Evolutionary Ethics*, ed. Matthew H. Nitecki and Doris V. Nitecki, 241–256. Albany: State University of New York Press.

Gilligan, Carol. 1982. *In a Different Voice: Psychological Theory and Women's Development.* Cambridge, Mass.: Harvard University Press.

Glanzer, M. 1953. Stimulus satiation: An exploration of spontaneous alteration and related phenomena. *Psychological Review* 60: 257–268.

Hart, H. L. A. 1968. *Punishment and Responsibility.* Oxford: Clarendon Press.

Hart, H. L. A. 1961. *The Concept of Law.* Oxford: Oxford University Press.

Held, Virginia. 1990. Feminist transformations of moral theory. *Philosophy and Phenomenological Research* 50 (Supplement, autumn):321–344.

Hinman, Lawrence M. 1979a. Can Skinner tell a lie? Notes on the epistemological nihilism of B. F. Skinner. *Southern Journal of Philosophy* 17:47–60.

Hinman, Lawrence M. 1979b. How not to naturalize ethics: The untenability of a Skinnerian naturalistic ethic. *Ethics* 89:292–297.

Hintz, Howard. 1958. Some further reflections on moral responsibility. In *Determinism and Freedom in the Age of Modern Science*, ed. Sidney Hook, 176–179. New York: New York University Press.

Hook, Sidney. 1958. Necessity, indeterminism, and sentimentalism. In *Determinism and Freedom in the Age of Modern Science*, ed. Sidney Hook, 180–192. New York: New York University Press.

Hospers, John. 1952. Free will and psychoanalysis. In *Readings in Ethical Theory*, ed. Wilfrid Sellars and John Hospers. New York: Appleton-Century-Crofts.

Hospers, John. 1958. What means this freedom. In *Determinism and Freedom in the Age of Modern Science*, ed. Sidney Hook, 126–142. New York: New York University Press.

James, William. 1897. The will to believe. In *The Will to Believe and Other Essays in Popular Philosophy*, 1–31. New York: Longmans, Green & Co.

Jeffers, Robinson. 1963. Their beauty has more meaning. In *Selected Poems*. New York: Random House.

Jonas, Hans. 1969. Philosophical reflections on experimenting with human subjects. In *Experimentation with Human Subjects*, ed. Paul A. Freund. New York: George Braziller.

Kane, Robert. 1985. *Free Will and Values*. Albany: State University of New York Press.

Kant, I. 1785/1949. *The Foundations of the Metaphysics of Morals*. In *The Philosophy of Immanuel Kant*. Trans. L. W. Beck. Chicago: University of Chicago Press, 1949.

Kavanau, J. Lee. 1967. Behavior of captive white-footed mice. *Science* 155:1623–1639.

Kleiman, Lowell. 1989. Morality as the best explanation. *American Philosophical Quarterly* 26:161–167.

Kuhn, Thomas S. 1962. *The Structure of Scientific Revolutions*. Chicago: University of Chicago Press.

Lakatos, Imre. 1978. *The Methodology of Scientific Research Programmes*, ed. John Worrall and Gregory Currie. Cambridge: Cambridge University Press.

Langton, Rae. 1992. Duty and desolation. *Philosophy* 67.

Llewelyn, J. E. 1966. The inconceivability of pessimistic determinism. *Analysis* 27:39–44.

Lewis, C. S. 1970. The humanitarian theory of punishment. In *Undeceptions*. London: Curtis Brown.

Lorenz, Konrad Z. 1952. *King Solomon's Ring*. New York: Thomas Y. Crowell Co.

Lumsden, C. J., and Wilson, E. O. 1981. *Genes, Mind and Culture: The Coevolutionary Process*. Cambridge, Mass.: Harvard University Press.

Lycan, William G. 1986. Moral facts and moral knowledge. *The Southern Journal of Philosophy* 24 (supplement):79–94.

MacIntyre, Alasdair. 1957. Determinism. *Mind* 66:28–41.

Mackie, J. L. 1982. Morality and the retributive emotions. *Criminal Justice Ethics* 1:3–10.

Mason, William A. 1993. The nature of social conflict: A psycho-ethological perspective. In *Primate Social Conflict*, ed. William A.

Mason and Sally P. Mendoza, 13–47. Albany: State University of New York Press.

Masserman, Jules H., Wechkin, Stanley, and Terris, William. 1964. 'Altruistic' behavior in rhesus monkeys. *American Journal of Psychiatry* 121:584–585.

McGinn, Colin. 1979. Evolution, animals and the basis of morality. *Inquiry* 22:84–98.

Mercer, Philip. 1972. *Sympathy and Ethics*. Oxford: Clarendon Press.

Midgley, Mary. 1994. *The Ethical Primate*. London: Routledge.

Midgley, Mary. 1989. *Wisdom, Information, and Wonder*. London: Routledge.

Midgley, Mary. 1978. *Beast and Man: The Roots of Human Nature*. Ithaca, N.Y.: Cornell University Press.

Moore, G. E. 1912. *Ethics*. London: Oxford University Press.

Morris, Herbert. 1968. Persons and punishment. *The Monist* 52: 475–501. (Page references as reprinted in *Punishment and Rehabilitation*, ed. Jeffrie G. Murphy. 2d. Ed. Belmont, Calif.: Wadsworth Publishing Co., 1985.)

Murdoch, Iris. 1971. *The Sovereignty of Good*. New York: Schocken.

Murphy, Jeffrie G. 1988. Hatred: A qualified defense. In *Forgiveness and Mercy*, ed. J. Murphy and Jean Hampton. Cambridge: Cambridge University Press.

Murphy, Jeffrie G. 1982. *Evolution, Morality, and the Meaning of Life*. Totowa, N.J.: Rowman and Littlefield.

Murphy, Jeffrie G. 1979. Marxism and retribution. In *Retribution, Justice, and Therapy*, ed. Jeffrie G. Murphy. Dordrecht, Holland: D. Reidel Publishing Co.

Nagel, Thomas. 1986. *The View from Nowhere*. New York: Oxford University Press.

Nagel, Thomas. 1978. Ethics as an autonomous theoretical subject. In *Morality as a Biological Phenomenon*, ed. Gunther S. Stent, 196–205. Berlin: Dahlem Konferenzen.

Oldenquist, Andrew. 1988. An explanation of retribution. *The Journal of Philosophy* 85:464–478.

Pound, Ezra. 1957. Sestina: Altaforte. In *Selected Poems of Ezra Pound*. New York: New Directions.

Povinelli, Daniel J., and Godfrey, Laurie R. 1993. The chimpanzee's mind: How noble in reason? How absent of ethics? In *Evolutionary Ethics*, ed. Matthew H. Nitecki and Doris V. Nitecki, 277–324. Albany: State University of New York Press.

Quine, Willard Van Orman. 1960. *Word & Object*. Cambridge, Mass: MIT Press.

Rachels, James. 1990. *Created From Animals*. Oxford: Oxford University Press.

Railton, Peter. 1986. Moral realism. *Philosophical Review* 45:163–207.

Ross, W. D. 1930. *The Right and the Good*. Oxford: The Clarendon Press.

Ruse, Michael. 1986. *Taking Darwin Seriously*. Oxford: Basil Blackwell.

Sackett, G. P. 1972. Exploratory behavior of rhesus monkeys as a function of rearing experiences and sex. *Developmental Psychology* 6:266–270.

Sayre-McCord, Geoffrey. 1988. Moral theory and explanatory impotence. In *Essays on Moral Realism*, ed. Geoffrey Sayre-McCord, 256–281. Ithaca, N.Y.: Cornell University Press.

Schlick, Moritz. 1939. When is a man responsible? In *Problems of Ethics*, ed. Moritz Schlick. Trans. David Rynin. Englewood Cliffs, N.J.: Prentice-Hall.

Seligman, Martin E. P. 1975. *Helplessness: On Depression, Development, and Death*. New York: W. H. Freeman.

Sesardic, Neven. 1995. Recent work on human altruism and evolution. *Ethics* 106:128–157.

Sher, George. 1987. *Desert*. Princeton, N.J.: Princeton University Press.

Singer, Peter. 1981. *The Expanding Circle*. New York: Farrar, Straus & Giroux.

Skinner, B. F. 1978. *Reflections on Behaviorism and Society*. Englewood Cliffs, N.J.: Prentice-Hall, Inc.

Skinner, B. F. 1974. *About Behaviorism*. New York: Alfred A. Knopf.

Skinner, B. F. 1971. *Beyond Freedom and Dignity*. New York: Alfred A. Knopf.

Skinner, B. F. 1969. *Contingencies of Reinforcement.* New York: Appleton-Century-Crofts.

Sober, Elliott. 1994. *From a Biological Point of View.* Cambridge: Cambridge University Press.

Sober, Elliott. 1993. Evolutionary altruism, psychological egoism, and morality: Disentangling the phenotypes. In *Evolutionary Ethics,* ed. Matthew H. Nitecki and Doris V. Nitecki, 199–216. Albany: State University of New York Press.

Stocker, Michael. 1976. The schizophrenia of modern ethical theories. *Journal of Philosophy* 63:453–466.

Strawson, P. F. 1962. Freedom and resentment. *Proceedings of the British Academy* 36.

Strier, K. B. 1992. Causes and consequences of nonaggression in the woolly spider monkey, or muriqui. In *Aggression and Peacefulness in Humans and Other Primates,* ed. J. Silverberg and J. P. Gray, 100–116. New York: Oxford University Press.

Suomi, S. J., and Harlow, H. F. 1976. The facts and functions of fear. In *Emotions and Anxiety: New Concepts, Methods, and Applications,* ed. M. Zuckerman and C. D. Speilberger. Hillsdale, N.J.: Lawrence Erlbaum Associates.

Taylor, Charles. 1976. Responsibility for self. In *Identities of Persons,* ed. Amelie Rorty, 281–299. Berkeley: University of California Press, 1976.

Taylor, Richard. 1963. *Metaphysics.* Englewood Cliffs, N.J.: Prentice-Hall.

Tolman, E. C. 1925. Purpose and cognition: The determiners of animal learning. *Psychological Review,* 32:285–297.

Toulmin, Stephen. 1970. Reasons and causes. In *Explanation in the Behavioural Sciences,* ed. Robert Borger and Frank Cioffi, 1–26. Cambridge: Cambridge University Press.

Trivers, Robert. 1971. The evolution of reciprocal altruism. *Quarterly Review of Biology* 46:35–57.

Van Inwagen, Peter. 1983. *An Essay on Free Will.* Oxford: Clarendon Press.

de Waal, Frans. 1996. *Good Natured: The Origins of Right and Wrong in Humans and Other Animals.* Cambridge, Mass.: Harvard University Press.

de Waal, Frans. 1989. *Peacemaking Among Primates*. Cambridge, Mass.: Harvard University Press.

de Waal, Frans. 1982. *Chimpanzee Politics*. London: Jonathan Cape.

Waller, Bruce N. 1990. *Freedom Without Responsibility*. Philadelphia: Temple University Press.

Waller, Bruce N. 1989. Denying responsibility: The difference it makes. *Analysis* 49:44–47.

Waller, Bruce N. 1988. Hard determinism and the principle of vacuous contrast. *Metaphilosophy* 19:65–69.

Waller, Bruce N. 1986. The virtues of contemporary emotivism. *Erkenntnis* 25:61–75.

Waller, Bruce N. 1985. Deliberating about the inevitable. *Analysis* 45:48–52.

Waller, Bruce N. 1982. Determinism and Behaviorist Epistemology. *Southern Journal of Philosophy* 20:513–532.

Wechkin, S., Masserman, J. H., and Terris, W. 1964. Shock to a conspecific as an aversive stimulus. *Psychonomic Science* 1:47–48.

Williams, Bernard. 1993. *Shame and Necessity*. Berkeley: University of California Press.

Williams, Bernard. 1985. *Ethics and the Limits of Philosophy*. Cambridge, Mass.: Harvard University Press.

Williams, Bernard. 1985/1995. How free does the will need to be? In *Making Sense of Humanity*. Cambridge: Cambridge University Press. Originally presented as the Lindley Lecture, University of Kansas, 1985.

Williams, Bernard. 1965/1973. Morality and the emotions, Inaugural Lecture, Bedford College, London. In *Problems of the Self*. Cambridge: Cambridge University Press, 1973.

Williams, Patricia. 1993. Can beings whose ethics evolved be ethical beings? In *Evolutionary Ethics*, ed. Matthew H. Nitecki and Doris V. Nitecki, 233–239. Albany: State University of New York Press.

Wilson, D. S. The group selection controversy: History and current status. *Annual Review of Ecology and Systematics* 14:159–187.

Wilson, D. S., and Sober, Elliott. 1994. Reintroducing group selection to the human behavioral sciences. *Behavioral and Brain Sciences* 17:585–654.

Wilson, Edward O. 1978. *On Human Nature.* Cambridge, Mass.: Harvard University Press.

Wilson, Edward O. 1975. *Sociobiology: The New Synthesis.* Cambridge, Mass.: Harvard University Press.

Wolf, Susan. 1990. *Freedom Within Reason.* Oxford: Oxford University Press.

Wolf, Susan. 1981. The importance of free will. *Mind,* 90:386–405.

Wolf, Susan. 1980. Asymmetrical freedom. *Journal of Philosophy,* 77. Page numbers as reprinted in John Martin Fischer (ed.), *Moral Responsibility,* 225–240. Ithaca, N.Y.: Cornell University Press, 1986.

Woolcock, P. 1993. Ruse's Darwinian Meta-Ethics: A Critique. *Biology and Philosophy* 8:423–439.

Zuckerman, Marvin. 1983. A biological theory of sensation seeking. In *Biological Bases of Sensation Seeking, Impulsivity, and Anxiety,* ed. Marvin Zuckerman, 37–76. Hillsdale, N.J.: Lawrence Erlbaum Associates.

# Index

## DATE DUE